A READING OF HENRY GREEN

A
READING
OF
HENRY
GREEN

By A. Kingsley Weatherhead

UNIVERSITY OF WASHINGTON PRESS

Seattle   1961

*This book is published with assistance
from a grant by the Ford Foundation.*

© *1961 by the University of Washington Press
Library of Congress Catalogue Card Number: 61-8767
Lithographed in the United States of America*

FOR INGRID

ACKNOWLEDGMENTS

Permission to quote from the following books is gratefully ac-
knowledged: from the works of Henry Green, *Blindness, Living,
Party Going, Pack My Bag, Caught, Loving, Back, Concluding,
Nothing, Doting,* The Viking Press, Inc.; from *Biographia
Literaria* by S. T. Coleridge, E. P. Dutton and Co., Inc.;
from *The Cocktail Party,* copyright 1950, by T. S. Eliot,
reprinted by permission of Harcourt, Brace and Company,
Inc.; from "East Coker" in *Four Quartets,* copyright 1943, by
T. S. Eliot, reprinted by permission of Harcourt, Brace and
Company, Inc.; from *Interpretation of Dreams,* by Sigmund
Freud, translated by A. A. Brill, George Allen and Unwin, Ltd.;
from *A Farewell to Arms,* by Ernest Hemingway, Charles
Scribner's Sons; from *The Intent of the Critic,* edited by
Donald A. Stauffer, Princeton University Press; from *Essays
in Pragmatism,* by William James, Hafner Publishing Com-
pany, Inc.; from *Lives of the Poets,* by Samuel Johnson, E. P.
Dutton and Co., Inc.; from *The Concept of Dread,* by Søren
Kierkegaard, translated by Walter Lowrie, Princeton Univer-
sity Press; from *Fear and Trembling and The Sickness Unto
Death,* by Søren Kierkegaard, translated by Walter Lowrie,
Princeton University Press; from *The Abolition of Man,* copy-
right 1943, by C. S. Lewis, The Macmillan Company; from
The Tightrope Walkers, by Giorgio Melchiori, Routledge and
Kegan Paul, Ltd.; from *Being and Nothingness,* by Jean-Paul
Sartre, translated by Hazel E. Barnes, Philosophical Library,
Inc.; from *Rehearsals of Discomposure,* by Nathan Scott,
Columbia University Press; from *Bread and Wine,* by Ignazio

Silone, translated by Gwenda David and Eric Mosbacher, Harper and Brothers; from *The Seed Beneath the Snow,* by Ignazio Silone, translated by Frances Frenaye, Harper and Brothers; from *The Liberal Imagination,* by Lionel Trilling, The Viking Press, Inc.; from *The English Novel: Form and Function,* by Dorothy Van Ghent, Rinehart and Company, Inc.

I am grateful for assistance from the librarians and their staffs at the University of Puget Sound and Louisiana State University in New Orleans and from Peter Johnson. For critical guidance, general and particular, I wish to thank James W. Hall, Arnold Stein, William Matchett, Harold P. Simonson, and my wife, Ingrid.

A. Kingsley Weatherhead

Eugene, Oregon
January, 1961

CONTENTS

A READING OF HENRY GREEN

1. INTRODUCTION

If we have been brought up on novels that scrupulously gratify the expectations they arouse, we may be dismayed by those of Henry Green. For these often leave us, with various loose ends in our hands, wondering just what happened or whether anything really happened at all. They would certainly dismay the man E. M. Forster envisages on the golf course. For what he wants, and his wife, too, is a "story"; and in these novels a story, in its most primitive and melodramatic sense, is what he will not get.

This study considers each of Green's novels and discovers some kind of order in the theme of self-creation. Characters emerge from childhood or other static situations, descend with whatever pains into the dark for the discovery of self, and break through alienation into community; or they partly proceed thus; or, faced with the opportunity, they altogether decline to. Then the order so discovered sometimes reveals in turn the significance of structures in the novels; and it offers a rationale for incident, imagery, and characters that are manifestly not of the "story" and do not contribute primarily to atmosphere.

In studying self-creation and its ramifying implications I have properly considered various aspects of the novels that have seemed either to be immediately relevant or to contribute from a distance to the theme in which I am interested. I have not considered all aspects of the novels: some, both large and small, I have consciously bypassed; and there are no doubt others which it has simply not occurred to me to discuss. The

3

study cannot therefore claim to be either a neutral or a complete critical assessment: it is a reading; and it is only one reading. Neither does it try to define the rare quality of Henry Green's art. Indeed, it speaks perhaps with too little enthusiasm of a literary genius which, when working well, is beyond praise.

This reading receives no appreciable direct contribution from any sources outside the texts of the novels themselves. A few critical essays, however, have been of indirect assistance: some have dealt usefully with topics that, while peripheral, are not alien to the central interest of this study; others, approaching Green more generally, have cleared ground and have even hinted at where the good things might be found. [1]

Still other essays, however, from the small body of criticism that exists, and certain reviews make other discoveries and contribute to readings of a different kind. I must notice in particular here the relatively large number of readings that rest upon the discovery of social allegory in the novels. If I have ignored the allegorical appearance of the larger social structures, I have done so because I am interested in another thing. By no means do I suppose my own reading to be incompatible with these others. Nevertheless it does seem to me that it is not the larger cultural aggregations, grist to the sociologists' mill, that Green wants to talk about most; and it is in accordance with this belief that I have disposed my emphasis. The larger structures certainly appear; they certainly provide milieu and tone. But Green's interest, I believe, is primarily directed toward the private movements of individuals within the group. He has pushed the generalization and the abstract or near abstract beyond the perimeter of his field (which is not to say he has retreated from them any more than to say he has advanced beyond them) and has focused down upon small concretions. And the direction his interest has taken has resulted in the brilliant exploration of the relationships of men and women to their real selves.

Certain of the reviews and critical essays that offer allegorical sociological readings are identified in the relevant places in the notes. Of such commentaries there is a significant number, and I do not prefer my own reading without due respect.

But in this connection I appeal to a good precedent for my inability to count heads.

Then, too, I have not made any unified comment upon the comedy of Green. Among the reviewers there is a general consensus that the novels, the later ones at least, are comic, brilliant, light, and witty; and the metaphors chosen to describe them, not unlike those conventionally applied to "The Rape of the Lock," are of jewelry, lacework, and bubbles. From this general voice I do not dissent. But it will appear, superficially, that where reviewers have reveled among iridescent pleasures, I, on the other hand, like an unbidden guest, have busied myself with images of hell and analogues of the dark night of the soul. The only reason, however, that in this study I do not discuss the brilliant comic effects except perhaps with a passing remark is that I am concerned with other affairs.

In the course of the study I have cited certain other novelists, contemporary with Green or earlier, whose interests and whose techniques in dealing with their interests are comparable. The purpose is to illuminate Green by comparison and not to allocate to him his correct place in the history of the novel. Some of the literature of philosophy and psychology, notably Kierkegaard, Sartre, and Freud, is also cited. Such literature either treats in abstraction some of the problems that Green has materialized or describes processes that are analogous to his techniques. I quote from this literature simply for the sake of illumination without suggesting that it influenced Green. Indeed, some of the novels antedate the relevant abstract material. Nor do I quote the other writers in the hope of proving anything about the novels; rather, the novels themselves, with their empirical data, may serve to support the abstract material.

The work proceeds by exploring the theme of self-creation in the novels in their chronological order. Under the heading of each of these are discussed the features most important to the novel under consideration and sometimes foreshadowings of features that become important in later novels. Sometimes, for instance, an explicitly expressed relationship in an earlier novel becomes a figurative one in a later; sometimes a rela-

tively slight tendency of style anticipates a large strategy.
The novels, however, are not necessarily treated exhaustively
each in its place; sometimes, for the sake of giving it a com-
parative treatment, the style of one novel is discussed under
the heading of another; sometimes less significant features
may be merely mentioned, to be accorded a fuller treatment
in the discussions of later novels where their more important
analogues appear. Then in the conclusion, which tries to take
a wide view of the novels as a whole, analogous features are
studied comparatively, some small observations are made
that could be included only awkwardly in the chapters, and one
or two general comments are very tentatively submitted.

2. BLINDNESS

Henry Green's first novel, *Blindness,* is both a natural and an easy way into the subject of self-creation. Its issues are clear and relatively uncompromised. Indeed, they are perhaps too straightforward: Green had not, we may assume, at the age of twenty when he wrote the novel, grasped the full complexity of the theme with which he was later to deal more sensitively. But the straightforwardness is useful to the reader, as the melodic initial statement of a musical theme is useful to the listener who must learn it well enough to know it later when it undergoes variation and is crossed and countercrossed by other motifs.

Since *Blindness* is out of print and virtually unobtainable, I shall summarize it briefly here. The novel describes the development of John Haye. The first part, thirty-four pages (there are 250 pages in all), consists entirely of unedited, intermittent diary entries, which the seventeen-year-old boy describes as "just a sort of pipe to draw off the swamp water."[1] The diary runs from July of one year to October of the next, his last academic year at Noat, an English public school. It shows more than anything else his sense of detachment from the other boys. This attitude becomes stronger when B. G. and Seymour, two boys of his own kind who with him constitute a minority clique, leave the school. His separateness, partly self-imposed and partly thrust upon him, and his iconoclasm are manifest in various incidents which it is unnecessary to detail here. It will, perhaps, suffice to say that his position in the school and his attitude to it resemble closely those

7

of Holden Caulfield in *The Catcher in the Rye.* Other things
in the diary reveal its writer's interest in books, especially
their prose style, his sincere desire to be a writer himself,
his self-awareness, his cultivated boredom at the school,
and his apathy toward its other pupils and all the conventional
values for which it stands and which it attempts to instill in
him.

The diary ends with a phrase that is part of a rhapsodic
note on *Crime and Punishment,* which John has just read:
"And the final episode, in Siberia, by the edge of the river
that went to the sea where there was freedom, reconciliation,
love.'"[2] Then follows, between Parts I and II, an extract from
a letter written by B. G. to Seymour telling him that John
has been blinded by the act of a small boy who had thrown a
stone and broken the train window against which he had been
standing.

Part II opens at Barwood, the Hayes' country estate. Here
we learn the effects of John's blindness of which the most immediate for both John and his stepmother is a sharpening of
the sense of distance between them. An observation made by
Mrs. Haye is indicative:

> "I am afraid I shall never be a good mother to you, John. I don't
> understand anything except out-of-door things, and babies. You
> were a lovely baby when you were small, and I could do every-
> thing for you then, and I loved it. But now you've outgrown me in
> a way and left me behind. . . . As I was saying to Mabel the other
> day, I don't understand the young generation."[3]

Mrs. Haye is perplexed about what to do for the boy, whose
father has been dead for some time. She is overwrought; but
she hangs on as best she can to the ordinary duties of her
everyday life, upbraiding her maid over the care of her clothes,
warning the gardener to prevent the stones in the grass from
breaking the blades of the mower, complaining about coffee, and whatever, for "the house must go on as usual."[4]
But although she busies herself about her immediate concerns, the disaster continually comes to mind. She regret-
fully discards the plans she had made for John's future and
for her own and tentatively suggests others to herself. But
she does so only halfheartedly, for again she realizes the

uncomfortable distance that separates her from the new generation.

For John himself the effects of the wound are many and
varied: the physical pain; the strong sense of his loss of the
natural world, birds and flowers, lines and colors; the feeling that this tragedy ought to have overtaken one of the "mud-
died oafs" at school; and, particularly, great resentment at
the small boy who had blinded him that finds outlet in a kind
of daydream in which he tortures this child to death and becomes a newspaper sensation.

He remains inactive during the first stage of his blindness.
He lies in the garden recollecting his former experiences of
the country. The images he evokes for himself are intense;
and they are stylized pictures rather than realities, frozen
tableaus flooded by an ideal light nostalgically engendered by
deprivation of the real.

> Flashes came back of things seen and remembered, but they
> were not clear-cut. Little bits in a wood, a pool in a hedge with
> red flowers everywhere, a red-coated man in the distance on a
> white horse galloping, the sea with violet patches over grey where
> the seaweed stained it, silver where the sun rays met it. A gull
> coming up from beneath a cliff. [5]

Or, recalling fishing, he imagines a "phantom-like" chub in
the "cloudy onyx of the water." [6]

The third and last chapter of Part II leaves John Haye in
this passive, withdrawn phase of "becoming" and turns to the
affairs of Joan Entwhistle and her father, who live squalidly
in a dilapidated cottage two miles from Barwood. The natural
setting of the cottage is idyllic; but Entwhistle, a gin-drinking,
defrocked vicar, resents the beauty of it. He feels that nature
smiles, ignoring his inner torment. And shut out from enjoying nature himself he feels alienated from those who do and
fulminates against the world. This dipsomaniacal failure is
engaged in writing an important book, engaged, at any rate,
in thinking about it, which is "to link everything into a circle."
Meanwhile Joan looks after him, dreaming dreams of marriage but knowing that such dreams will never be fulfilled because of her duties to her father.

A large part of this chapter is devoted to Joan's nostalgic

memories of the beautiful past when the Entwhistles were
still respectable and had the vicarage and a garden, before
they were overtaken by calamity, as crippling to Joan as his
blindness to John. Of the earlier life the dominant image is
that of the roses which her father had assiduously cultivated
despite the cost, until their expensive treatment had been curtailed in order to buy gin.

In Part II Joan had cut her thumb opening a can of sardines.
In Part III Mrs. Haye meets her in the lane and insists on her
coming to the house to have the wound treated.

> So they [Joan and John] had met. But Mamma's voice had been
> uneasy all through her account of it; she had been frightened. She
> had told him that artists married barmaids continually and were
> unhappy ever after. And he had said that unhappiness was neces-
> sary to artists, and she had called that stuff and nonsense. But
> they had met.[7]

By this time John has begun to orient himself in relation to
his blindness. He tends now to perceive nature in auditory
images rather than conceive it in recollected visual ones. He
finds his sense of hearing sharpened. "Sight," he decided
moreover, "was not really necessary; the values of everything changed, that was all."[8] This rehabilitation is helped by
his growing acquaintance with Joan. They go for walks together; and with forced compatibility they indulge in staccato
dialogues in which John insists on calling her "June." In these
dialogues we hear again of John's determination to be a writer,
and then of his intention to go to live in London.

John soon tires of Joan, however. In one disconsolate scene
she pleads to go to the city with him and he unwillingly agrees
to take her. But then she will not go: she has read a novel
about the infidelity of the artist type; and furthermore, she
cannot leave her father, she explains, although from time to
time he attacks her brutally. She weeps at John's decision to
leave; then when he offers to stay she tearfully insists that he
go. But after they part, Joan retreats to an improved relationship with her father and a happier acceptance of her lot.

John's desire to go to London presents Mrs. Haye with a
conflict between her duty toward the village and that to her
stepson, which is eventually resolved in John's favor. But in
London, John's blindness becomes once again a disability, for

the house and streets are hostile to his ear and, temporarily at least, he thinks longingly of Barwood. He imagines all Barwood laughing at him for going away to discover how helpless he is. Nevertheless he maintains his determination to write and to look forward rather than back; he sneers at his stepmother because she talks with her friend of things past while "June and he had carved great slices out of the future."[9]

Finally, in the last pages of the novel, in a kind of fit of ecstasy, he is filled with a strong sense of "becoming." He strains upward toward a great white light of knowledge. And finally, back in the world again, he feels able to write.

These are the main incidents of *Blindness*; and the titles of the three parts, "Caterpillar," "Chrysalis," and "Butterfly," indicate its concern with development. Certain aspects of the adolescent struggle that show John Haye contending with the inevitable concomitants of development may now be profitably discussed in the light of Kierkegaard's *Concept of Dread* and in its terms.

John's diary shows his unwillingness to settle for conventional attitudes and a determination to realize and develop what is individual in himself. Now the goal of personality development, according to Kierkegaard, is freedom; and the possibility of freedom brings dread.[10] In the novel, that state of normal dread which in individual human histories accompanies the process of the actualization of selfhood, what modern psychology calls anxiety, is objectified in John Haye by blindness. And if blindness seems a terrible wound by which to figure dread, still it is less terrible than the inquisitorial torture in terms of which Kierkegaard describes it.[11]

Dread differs from fear, in that a man turns away from fear but embraces his dread. "A situation provokes fear," says Sartre, "if there is a possibility of my life being changed from without; my being provokes anguish [dread] to the extent that I distrust myself and my own reactions in that situation."[12] Now clearly it is unscientific to read John Haye's blindness as an anguish provoked by himself; it has a very concrete cause in the external world, no less susceptible to scientific description than the onset of little Hanno's typhus in *Buddenbrooks*. Two qualifications must be made, however: first, as will be discussed more fully in a later chapter, what is essentially internal must discover external embodiment for dramatic purposes; and second, John's salvation demands that he regard his blindness *as if it were not* essentially external, following a hint in the diary which suggests that it had always been an inherent possibility. "Rather a funny thing happened while fielding this afternoon. I had thrown myself down to stop a ball and I saw waving specks in my eyes for two minutes afterwards. I suppose my blood pressure was disturbed. "[13] The attitude toward the wound that conceives it as not essentially external will, when he achieves it, be a recognition in private terms that the evil of the world is within him. And such recognition is a fundamental condition for growth.

Meanwhile John's first reaction is rebellious. He regards the wound only as the result of an arbitrary, external act and curses its agent, the small boy. He has to learn to conceive of it as part of the process of self-creation, to understand that "our only health is the disease." On the other hand he must not hug his wound; he must and eventually does achieve the relationship described by Kierkegaard as "sympathetic and antipathetic. "[14]

He is but vaguely aware of the process he is undergoing: "'I think perhaps suffering is rather fine, don't you?' Was it? He did not know. At any rate, it was a way out of blindness. "[15] Nevertheless, he comes to such terms with his blindness that he is able to accept what is virtually a re-enactment of the wounding process when his development demands the move to London and his blindness is in a sense renewed.

The self that would develop on lines of its own unique possibilities is threatened by the attraction exerted by patterns, either those laid down by convention or those simply at hand in another person. The conventional waiter described by Gabriel Marcel is an excellent example of the dominating stereotype. John Haye's development is threatened first by the conventions of his school, which he must flaunt, and second, and more significantly though of the same order, by the role his stepmother wishes him to play.

Mrs. Haye's expectations of him fall naturally within the narrow limits of her own imagination which in turn is limited by her own and her late husband's role. Her husband had been an army officer; her own role is that of the benevolent, auto-

cratic manager of all the affairs of the village. In such terms
she makes plans for John. "Plans must be made for when his
new life would begin, and some idea might emerge out of her
work. Being blind he could do work for the other blind, and
so not feel solitary, but get *the feeling of a regiment*."[16] Passages detailing her plans for him to marry, to maintain the hall,
to take up where she left off in the affairs of the village are
too long to be quoted. Two passages, however, will show how
John's struggle consists not merely in avoiding his stepmother's advice but in escaping her possession of him. In the first,
the error of thinking "her" instead of "him," indicating her
tendency to identify herself with John, suggests the extent of
his danger.

> But then he didn't hunt, he didn't shoot, he only fished and that
> sitting down, and he couldn't fish now. Perhaps it was just as well
> he had given up huntin' it would have been terrible had that been
> taken away from her suddenly.[17]

> It was all part of this modern spirit, she had seen terrible dan-
> gers there for him, but now, poor boy, that he was blind she could
> at least keep him to herself away from those things that led no-
> where.[18]

John's victory over his stepmother is finally achieved when
he forces her to sell Barwood in order that he may live in London. For he must leave Barwood, although his life there has
become little short of idyllic and although "in the·country you
had been able to forget that you were blind."[19] He must leave
it not only on account of the threat of possession but because
the country represents an early stage through which he must
pass in the process of growth. The country, the garden in particular with obvious echoes of *the* Garden, becomes in Green
a metaphor for early innocence and ignorance. John's departure from it involves a renewal of blindness. And once again
in London, the wrong, stagnating attitude of mere rebellion
against fate has to be overcome. "That child on the platform
as they had been coming up here: 'Look, Mumma, . . . blind,
Mumma,' and the horror which had been in its little cursed
treble because another little thing had thrown a stone at a passing train. Of course it had been his window the stone hit, of
course."[20]

Up to this point the wound in *Blindness* has been read as an objectification of dread. It must be considered, however, as the objectification of other adversities associated with growth. The policy of embodying various adversities in a single figure is manifestly apt. For John Haye is immature; and the inability to discriminate between different qualities of pleasure or pain is an index of the immature, sentimental mind.

Guilt then, of which the relation to dread is clear neither to Kierkegaard nor to contemporary psychologists, is embodied along with it in the figure of blindness. Guilt is associated with self-creation because the latter involves the destruction of whatever opposes it—the *status quo* and its conventional patterns. Artistic creativity, which is a more intense form of self-creation, manifests guilt to a more intense degree. And both painters and writers have attested to feelings of inexplicable guilt.

The inexplicability of this guilt is due to its lack of conscious content. The artist or the developing individual *feels* guilty but does not necessarily know why. Thus the overt sense of guilt in John Haye is minimal; there are merely two short passages in which he questions whether he ought to have dragged his mother away from Barwood and whether he ought to have left Joan.

It is of course significant that the sense of guilt is related to the parent and to the girl, who is also in a sense a mother figure. The guilt is covertly related to the father against whose way of life and values the protagonist revolts. One is reminded of other literary figures, contemporary and ancient: Stephen Dedalus, in *A Portrait of the Artist as a Young Man,* who rejected his father and manifested guilt feelings in relation to his mother since fidelity to his own self-creation prevented his kneeling at her deathbed; Joseph, in *Joseph in Egypt,* who, for the greater purpose, departed from his father and embraced foreign manners; Meursault, in *The Stranger,* who rejected such conventional values as adhered to by the prosecutor, the father figure, and was condemned to death for his guilt toward his mother. And one is reminded of Oedipus.

The association between guilt and self-creation, particularly artistic creation, and the statement of Kierkegaard that "the greater the genius the more profoundly he discovers guilt"[21] invite the question whether John Haye's guilt, which is manifest as a wound, is a form of suffering useful to him as a writer. The general question is discussed by Lionel Trilling in his criticism of the dominant concept of Edmund Wilson's *The Wound and the Bow*. Although it is not his final finding, Trilling posits the possibility that

> By means of his belief in his own sickness, the artist may the more easily fulfill his chosen, and assigned, function of putting himself into connection with the forces of spirituality and morality; the artist sees as insane the "normal" and "healthy" ways of established society, while aberration and illness appear as spiritual and moral health if only because they controvert the ways of respectable society. [22]

John Haye's statement, on the other hand, is final: "He had said that unhappiness was necessary to artists."[23] Suffering in the form of blindness, however, is at first an impediment to John Haye, as artist, who seeks to write about the life of the city streets. But it apparently becomes something else. John notices in the first place a compensatory sharpening of his other senses. Then, about halfway through the book, a compensation other than this familiar physiological phenomenon is indicated: "There was so much to find out, and, in a sense, so much to discover for others, for when one was blind one understood differently. A whole set of new values had arisen."[24] Again, almost at the end of the novel, is a passage in which "aberration and illness appear as spiritual and moral health if only because they controvert the ways of respectable society." "It was the easiest thing in the world to see, and so very many were content with only the superficial appearance of things; it would teach them so much if they were to go blind. . . ."[25]

My interest in this motif in *Blindness* is not for the support it gives to Wilson's implicit theses. The last words of the book, in a letter to B. G. written after John's recovery from his fit, say, "'I have had such a wonderful experience. I am going to settle down to writing now. . . .'" The "experience" here was the inward ecstasy: "He was rising through the mist, blown on a gust of love, lifting up, straining at a white light that he would bathe in. . . . And when he had bathed there he would know all, why he was blind, why life had been so to him."[26]

What has happened to John is that his blindness in denying

external adventure has forced him to inward exploration. Privation of literal light has endowed him at length with the metaphorical light of self-knowledge. Or purgation, by privation
of self-in-the-world, has brought about inward experiences
that are preliminary to the actualization of self. Or a partial
death to the world has brought more abundant life. And so his
suffering, insofar as it promotes self-knowledge, is useful
to him.

The theme of this aspect of John Haye's career is worth
playing with variations; for many of Green's characters undergo analogous metamorphoses for which certain of the above
terms are good. Although in no other novel is the darkness
absolute as it is in this one, characters in all of them depart
from the presence of rich, intensely lighted images into varying degrees of darkness; and the metaphorical significance
of their descent, as adumbrated in *Blindness*, is of particular interest.

It may be useful here to consider very briefly the career
of Joan Entwhistle which in many respects offers a contrast
to that of John Haye. Joan is unable to develop, arrested by
her loyalty to her father. Just as a wound gives John an en-
trée into a life of better values, so her wound, her cut thumb,
is the means by which she enters the environment of John and
is faced with an opportunity for self-development with all its
risks. But she repudiates the opportunity because of her father;
and her sacrifice of selfhood for him is only heroic in the sentimental appraisal that would make Dedalus, Joseph, and
Meursault villains. In fact she is only very slightly jealous of
her selfhood and puts up little resistance when John insists on
calling her "June" instead of "Joan."

Her life with her father is no idyl; she bears scars of wounds
inflicted by him with a broken bottle when he was drunk. A
possible figurative meaning for these wounds is suggested
below; meanwhile, we may notice that her reaction to them is
not that ambivalent one of John Haye, but one of morbid delight. Fingering her scars, she muses, "It had been wonderful that night. You felt a slave, a beaten slave."[27] And this
sickly attitude is that of the nauseating little man in Auden's
"Letter to a Wound."

Now just as self-creation brings guilt in its train, so too

does the refusal to grow. This kind of guilt is best exemplified
by the nameless guilt of Joseph K. in *The Trial*. By social and
ethical standards Joseph K.'s conduct is irreproachable: he
is the junior manager of a large bank and is most respectable;
he pays his debts and lives in sobriety. Nevertheless in fail-
ing to integrate divine demands with his development he has
stopped short in the full actualization of the possibility of selfhood. And when once he is "arrested" his conscience, which
is aware of the profound guilt while his conscious mind is not,
destroys his peace forever.[28] Such is the guilt of Joan Entwhistle which I take her wounds to objectify.

Finally, Joan may be contrasted to John in her reaction
to darkness. For she too, insofar as she has left the rose
garden of the vicarage, has descended a little way into a kind
of darkness. But then unlike him she has made peace with
privation, thus annulling its purgative effect. In this respect,
she is the forerunner of characters in the later novels who
are guilty of making hell soothing.

As for John, one further concomitant of self-creation that
blindness figures has not yet been discussed. His wound is
susceptible of an interpretation additional to, not replacing, the
ones already submitted. Blindness, which isolates its victim,
is a particularly apt symbol for alienation.

Alienation, which Kierkegaard calls "shut-upness," inhibits
freedom and the creation of self. At the same time, alienation is the particular characteristic of the aspirant pursuing
selfhood as he quits the crowd for the howling desert. Or
rather, forced upon him as he pursues freedom is the awareness of an alienation that had always existed. For all men
endure "the inescapable loneliness of the human soul" while
only some are aware of it, and of these only a few express
their awareness.

Among the more interesting discussions of alienation is
that of Nathan Scott. He suggests first that the tyrannical values of modern society have affected men of sensibility and
virtually exiled them from the community.[29] By "men of sensibility" he presumably means artists, since the people he names
as such are artists. Now whether John Haye is an artist, as
William York Tindall suggests, [30] or whether he is one of the
many, familiar to the trustees of fellowships, who "always

wanted to write a novel, " may not be ascertained on the available evidence. Certainly he is not insensible. But in any event,
Henry Green is an artist. And while we may not trespass into
biography to question the extent to which *Blindness* expresses
the author's own alienation, we may observe that the good
artist, according to Scott, as he becomes aware of his alienation realizes its universality. "The writers who seem to bring
most to us today are those who . . . so universalize their individual experience as to project a fundamental and radical
criticism of contemporary history." Sherwood Anderson, Scott
continues, is thus no longer significant, because, embracing
spiritual exile, he divorced himself from his community and
merely dramatized his own loneliness.[31]

Green's procedure is otherwise. Throughout the novels, because alienation is the universal lot, it afflicts all kinds of
men and women whether or not they are people of sensibility.
But we may question whether by the time of *Blindness* Green
had realized the universality of alienation. For though the
theme spills over from the story of John Haye, its principal
vessel, into that of Mr. Entwhistle, the latter may be roughly
classified with John as a man of sensibility. He is at least
thinking of writing a book.

In other respects he is signally different from John. Exile
is inflicted upon him as blindness is inflicted upon John. But
whereas John, as we shall see, reacts properly to alienation,
taking positive steps toward an environment where he can
break out of his aloneness, Entwhistle, cursing his environment, merely idles away his life in the inactive flattery of
his purely imaginary genius.

Nathan Scott describes the members of the contemporary
community as being estranged from the cultural tradition,
from themselves, and from love. Love, since it is the means
of communion that does not compromise selfhood, is the means
by which Green's protagonists in general tend to deal with
their alienation. But John Haye in *Blindness* deals with it predominantly in terms consonant with the metaphor, "shut-
upness." "The shut-up is precisely the mute," says Kierkegaard, "the spoken word is precisely the saving thing."[32]
John's dialogues with Joan are stiff and forced, but they provide the necessary vehicle for expression. Later and more

significantly, we understand that he is to engage in literary composition which is both a means of communion and an expression of self. Entwhistle's alienation also takes the form of muteness, and expression is posited as a way out of it. At one time he rationalizes that he must take gin in order to be able to write his book; the passage ends, "How ill he felt. . . . Why could not the doctors do something about it? *Oh, for a pulpit to say it from.*"[33]

John Haye's success in managing his alienation is unduly complete, and *Blindness* ends on a note of almost complete triumph. John is prepared to write; the schoolboy dream has apparently come true, and his happiness is unqualified. This ending implies among other things total victory over alienation and provides a strong conclusion. Such finality is uncommon in Green's later novels, and the defeat of alienation where it is a problem is less absolute. What we find in them and among the novels of his contemporaries is an exploration of the condition, a continuing struggle, or at best a partial victory.

The Castle is perhaps the novel that best illustrates the condition of alienation. And the novel is unfinished. K. has attempted and failed to annihilate the distance between himself and the castle. From the example of others he has learned some things concerning the terms of the endeavor, but at the point where the writing ceases he is still living in the village.

Similarly, *The Sun Also Rises* illustrates a palliation of alienation rather than a cure. The affliction is objectified in Jake Barnes, the protagonist, by impotence. It is significant to him only insofar as it precludes sexuality with Lady Brett Ashley; for in communion with her he could have discovered his real self from which he is isolated. In other relationships he is successful, just as Joseph K. in *The Trial* is socially successful. What happens in *The Sun Also Rises* is not such a gradual annihilation of his isolation on the part of the hero as is found in *Blindness*. Jake Barnes follows another pattern: he explores his situation and the respective possibilities of substitute passions and comes in the end to more or less unsatisfactory terms with his condition.

This pattern, because it is inconclusive, seems to be the right one for the problem in which it seeks to find order. By comparison, *Blindness*, in this particular and in some others,

must strike us as uncritically conclusive. A man may register
an occasional ephemeral victory in a local skirmish of a cam-
paign that can never be finally decided. But, even though a
boy's victories are more triumphant than a man's, the glorious achievement of John Haye is unreal. In Green's later
novels the success his characters achieve in dealing with their
isolation is much less sure.

Nevertheless, the inevitability with which obstacles are
duly overcome, the very thoroughness and the completion of
the procedure offer a fine, clear, if hypothetical paradigm
of the process of self-creation. The candidate, John Haye, is
willing: from the very first in his diary he shows his protes-
tantism. Though initially overwhelmed by dread in the violent
form it assumes, he comes before long to manage it. At a
price he resolutely discards his childhood. Then the darkness
of privation bears as its first fruits the beginnings of self-
knowledge. And finally he defeats his loneliness in literary expression.

3. LIVING

As the problem of alienation is somewhat easily disposed of in *Blindness,* so the larger problem of development and self-creation in the image of self, a process of which the defeat of alienation is a part, is too easily solved. At the end of the novel John Haye has some kind of fit in which there is a vision of knowledge; and even after the ecstasy is over he is thrilled with a sense of triumph uncompromised by his return to the world. With this the book ends, conventionally enough, and we leave him happy ever after. But the dream come true at the snap of the wizard's fingers, while suitable enough for the conventional novel, is a short cut across complexities; for the bright adolescent ideal is more or less tarnished when in real life it is forced to encounter the world and adapt itself to the claims and stringencies of actuality.

In the more realistic novel, *Living,* therefore, which is concerned with living in the real world and dreaming beyond it, we may expect to find some tension. The problem, of course, which John Haye is not made to face, is what to do with the vision. For the vision, which when preciously nourished precludes growth, cannot in itself be put to work in the world. Joan Entwhistle, who is only a minor figure embodying a minor motif, deals with her small vision by repudiating it entirely. Her action, if not heroic, is far from contemptible; it is merely normal. Large or small the vision can be disposed of. "If that is what you wish," says Sir Henry Harcourt-Reilly to Miss Coplestone in *The Cocktail Party:*

I can reconcile you to the human condition,
The condition to which some who have gone as far as you
Have succeeded in returning. They may remember
The vision they have had, but they cease to regret it,
Maintain themselves by the common routine,
Learn to avoid excessive expectation,
Become tolerant of themselves and others,
Giving and taking, in the usual actions
What there is to give and take.

The peace, however, that Lily Gates finally makes with her dreams in *Living* is neither that of the dream come true nor that of the dream entirely repudiated; it is the middle, complex situation of the dream trimmed down and accommodated to actuality. The main business of the novel is the conflict between the visions of the young and diurnal necessity, which exists to a certain extent in the constraints exerted by old men and their fixed, outdated patterns. Lily Gates's life in the real world consists of caring for her father, her grandfather, and the lodger Jim Dale in the grandfather's house. The dull, static routine of it is not to be questioned, for upon the fact that it has always been what it now is rests its inviolability. "'In this 'house,'" says Mr. Craigan, "'the wage earners must 'ave hot meals every night bar Fridays, if they don't come back midday for it. And on Saturdays there is to be two 'ot meals, and one on Sunday.'"[1] Her tedious life, set in the dreary milieu of industrial Birmingham, is controlled by such rules.

There is some limited escape for her in the Sunday sixpenny bus ride to the Lickeys, where "they keep the roads beautiful with the grass in between them and the trams going one road and cars t'other," and where "you can get right out into the country and get the fresh air."[2] And then occasionally there is the cinema for her, where within the permissive aura of exotic scenes and erotic music she can dream wild dreams.

Her dreams naturally carry her away beyond the confines of her status: sexual consummation, which in later novels becomes a kind of synecdoche for growth, plays a larger role in *Living* than it had in *Blindness,* and Lily sees herself with a man of her own and children to cherish in the never-never

country overseas. But when in the short-lived flight with Bert
Jones she seeks to realize these dreams, they evade her. The
excursion was not at all what she had expected. From the train
that is to take them to foreign places she sees the ordinary
native dress of an English girl and is tempted by a nostalgic
yearning for the stasis and its attendant security which she
associates with such clothes. Next she encounters the horrors
of anxiety and guilt, objectified first in almost arbitrarily selected objects that she sees during the journey: the bunch of
tulips, and the green muffler of the member of the band. When
they arrive in Liverpool, a city no less squalid than the one
they have left, anxiety and guilt are objectified in the night-
marish phantasmagoria of the dark slum streets.

When she returns home, she tells Mr. Craigan, "'I do wish
we 'adn't gone. '"

> "You were dreamin'. "
> "Yes grandad. "
> 'Nothin' ever come of dreams like them kind, " he said. "Nothin'
> dain't ever come of dreams, I could 'ave told yer but that wouldn't
> be of no use, you 'ad to find out of yourselves and so you 'ave, " he
> said. [3]

But Lily's dream is not entirely untranslatable into its realistic equivalents. Early in the novel there is a small symbolic
scene in which a sparrow is caught between the window frames
in the Craigan house. The three men are unable to free it, so
they send for their neighbor, Mrs. Eames, who immediately
releases it. Thus it is that later Mrs. Eames is able, where
the men are not, to offer Lily something of the freedom, freedom now in the sense of self-development, that her dreams
had envisaged. The vision of self as mother, although impossible to actualize fully, finds some small enactment when Mrs.
Eames allows Lily to push the pram with the new baby in it.
And for Lily, who by this time has learned the stoic's prayer,
"Make us not fly to dreams, but moderate desire, " the "sight
of baby blowing bubbles on her mouth . . . was moment of
utter bliss. "[4]

Lily is not the only character in the novel who fosters a
vision. In other men and women the idea of withdrawal to find
freedom in one form or another is enacted or more often en-

tertained. Herbert Tomson, for instance, announces to Bert
Jones, who tells Aaron Connolly who tells Mr. Eames and
Bert Jones again, that he is going to Australia. Bert Jones
himself entertains the idea of going to Canada. There are
minor ways, too, in which characters may get away from the
dominating workaday world or at least forget it for a time.
The continual retreat to the lavatory in the factory is a small
bid for temporary freedom; there is tennis for Tarver and
the Berlin radio concerts for Craigan. Often the attention of
characters is drawn to the processes and objects of nature
which may be observed even in the urban situation: the birth
of children and the associated joy, the birds, the growth of
plants, flowers turning their faces to the sun. And then by
means of passion, even the diurnal necessity itself, that which
is to be withdrawn from, may assume a romantic, visionary
appearance, as in this beautifully perceptive passage:

> As they walked, then Mr. Jones had rush of feeling. He saw
> everything one way. "Us working people we got to work for our liv-
> ing, " he said passionately, "till we're too old. It's no manner of
> use thinking about it, it's like that, right on till we're too old for
> them to use us. Then our children 'll make provision for us, " he
> said and stopped and suddenly he kissed her for the first time. She
> pressed up to his face, her eyes shining. Then for a long time they
> kissed each other, murmuring and not hearing what they murmured,
> behind cattle shed in field they had been crossing. [5]

The instinct to withdraw is not merely an esthetic urge to
get away from the squalid urban situation; in most cases it
is the urge to get away from the crowd in order to create the
self along its own unique lines. The motif is reiterated in Lily
when she asks, "'we shan't be like the others, Bert?'";[6] and
then again, "'Oh Bert we shan't be like the others shall we
dear?'" she says and listens reassured while he tells her how
different he is from the rest. And, after her nightmare which
presents the romantic dream of love and its fruits as a gray
reality of procreation, "she cried in her, I, I am I. "[7]

It is interesting to notice that for the adolescents in *Living*
and for their idealism the author shows a controlled sympathy
that is almost entirely withheld from the adolescents in subsequent novels. Lily's prayer shows a tenderness that is both
a remarkable departure from the over-all tone of the novel

and, looked at with hindsight after a consideration of later ones, a contrast in the treatment of adolescence.

> Lord give me a child that I might wash him, feed him, give him life. Yes let him be a boy. Give him blue eyes, let him cling to me with his hands and never be loosed from me. Give him me to love that I'm always kissing him and working for him. I've had nothing of my own. Give him me and let him be mine, oh, oh give me a life to work for, and give me the love of him, and his father's. [8]

The quality of the author's attitude toward Lily's dream, to the dream in general for that matter, is illuminated when the above passage is compared with the following gratuitous and savage satire on the self-satisfied lower *bourgeoisie* who have no dreams.

> Some of them have little jolly card parties with a few jolly fellows. They may be coming walking back from it. . . . By gad didn't know it was so late well better be getting along now or the wife won't have it eh, think I'm up to some of the old games what well old chap I'll say goodnight now oh I say no I say old man did you see your wife give me a kiss well perhaps it was a good thing you didn't. . . . [9]

The young people's dreams are thwarted not only negatively by their inherent incompatibility with the world but positively by the opposition of old men. In *Blindness,* there is a hint of the serious obstruction to the process of self-creation that is offered by the father figure; but John Haye's father had been dead fifteen years when blindness afflicted his son, and his opposition to John's progress appears only at second hand as it influences his stepmother's program for him. But in *Living,* the cast of which consists almost entirely of men and women in or near their adolescence and men well beyond middle age, the various father figures present strong opposition to the development of the young.

Toward Mr. Craigan, her grandfather, Lily shows the traditionally ambivalent attitude toward the father figure: love and a desire for his protection, on the one hand, and hostility and the urge to escape that protection, on the other. It is Gates's blow that actually provokes her departure from the house and it is to Craigan that she returns penitent. But her grandfather's protection, amounting to possession, is the chief factor in her discontent with her status.

Craigan is a father figure for others too: for Jim Dale, in particular, who succeeds in making a clean and complete break from him, and for the other factory workers. His paternal relationship to the workers is dramatized in the general excitement, the mingled respect and wish fulfillment, that follows his narrow escape from death in the factory. Joe Gates tells the incident to Lily, and Bert tells Jim Dale who, since he already knew, responds with more details; Tupe tells an unnamed young man, and Archer tells young Dupret. Bridges, however, is the chief father figure in the factory and so styles himself. He stands for authority and curtails the freedom and loose discipline of the men. And the hostility toward him is overt.

The conflict with the father figure is more important, however, in the part of the novel not yet considered that deals with young Dupret. In an upper class milieu Dick Dupret suffers and enjoys as do the young people in the Birmingham slum who have already been mentioned. Like them he has the urge to withdraw to the little place he knows of; although what he is withdrawing from, his real world of dinners, dances, and houseparties, is ironically the very content of the dreams of the lower order. Like Lily, he despises the crowd, which he immediately associates with Bridges and Walters, forces hostile to his own self-definition: "Both these [Bridges and Walters] were old, old. How horrible they all were and everyone too for that matter, loathsome the people in buses, worse in trams of course. . . ."[10]

Bridges and Walters, old members of the firm, bound by loyalty to Dupret senior, are, of course, father figures to Dick; and they offer what opposition they can when he takes steps to assert his authority in the firm, and they thereby impede his development. But the most crippling impediment is offered either deliberately or fortuitously by his actual father. Dupret senior, sick enough to have delegated his authority to Dick, is an unconscionable time dying; and while his collapse causes the cancellation of a ball and the interruption of Dick's romance with Hannah Glossop, before he dies he rallies sufficiently to reverse his son's decisions in the factory. His son's death wish for him is vociferous and undisguised: "Doctors said was no hope for him now. He felt he could go up now to room and say 'die, old fool, die.'"[11]

The young in every case are anxious to graduate immediately from the inhibitory, fatherly protection of their elders and to inherit an unchartered, protestant freedom. Their instincts are those of the migrant birds which strike mild fear into would-be possessors. "As these birds would go where so where would this child go?" the epigraph of the novel, is one of the thoughts of Mrs. Eames, as she watches migrating birds and associates them with her own unborn child.

The career of only one young person in the novel, Lily, is followed to any length. And the freedom Lily finally discovers is not unchartered: she returns from her flight to Mr. Craigan's protection, rooted in which she brings to fruition whatever of her dreams she may. What she achieves is not the freedom of the migrant birds but that of the pigeons. In the train while actually escaping him she thinks of Mr. Craigan, and the relationship between them is described in a Homeric simile:

> For as racing pigeon fly in the sky, always they go round above house which provides for them or, if loosed at a distance from that house then they fly straight there, so her thoughts would not point away long from house which had provided for her. With us it is not only food, as possibly it is for pigeon, but if we are for any length of time among those who love us and whom we love too, then those people become part of ourselves.
>
> As, in Yorkshire, the housewives on a Sunday will go out, in their aprons, carrying a pigeon and throw this one up and it will climb in spirals up in the air, then, when it has reached a sufficient height it will drop down plumb into the apron she holds out for it, so Miss Gates, in her thoughts and when these ever threatened to climb up in air, was always coming bump back again to Mr. Craigan.[12]

The freedom of the pigeon is the kind of freedom achieved by Lily's thoughts and subsequently by Lily when she finds the satisfaction of the dream within the terms of necessity. The freedom is limited: it will allow the birds their flight and Lily a degree of dream fulfillment. But it will not liberate either from the demands of the earth. The rather long pas-

sage about the pigeon is quoted here in full because the pigeons that frequently appear in later novels are more or less
susceptible to the figurative extension that Green makes perfectly explicit in *Living* [13]

The inhibitory effect of protective love is not suffered only
by the young at the hands of the old. In *Living* it works both
ways; Lily, for-example, although passively, comes to exert
a possessive influence on Craigan and, again passively, is
the one who determines the final arrangement of the household affairs, including those of her father. Possessive love
with infringement of freedom may be inflicted voluntarily or
otherwise by one young person on another; thus Jim Dale is
possessed by Lily, Hannah Glossop by Tyler, Dick Dupret
by Hannah Glossop: "Why, he asked in mind, should you leave
your life about to be cut in pieces by Miss Glossop."[14] Or
again possession may be inflicted by one old person on another
as it is by Dupret senior on his wife.

The case of Mrs. Dupret illustrates a theme of considerable importance, treated variously in nearly all Green's novels. Mr. Dupret had always done all her thinking for her.

> Then, while he had been so ill, she had been forced into being prac-
> tical to a certain degree, and now, as he seemed to become daily
> more and more competent to deal with what was about him, so her
> sanity, what there was of it, so it ebbed and she was drifting back
> again. . . . [15]

In Green there is an intimate connection between being practical and maintaining sanity; and thus conversely the deprivation of the opportunity for practical action is an injury. The
connection is merely glanced at in *Blindness* where immediately after the boy's disaster the overwrought Mrs. Haye seeks
stability by directing as usual the immediate daily affairs
of the estate. [16] In *Living* there are two or three instances
where work is viewed as mental therapy. It is good for Mrs.
Dupret, and it is prescribed for Hannah Glossop when the death
of the doctor's chauffeur causes her irrational distress. And
there is Dick Dupret who, dropped by Hannah, needs some
situation, something more than the London office where he
only signs checks, that will submit itself to his activities. It
is for this reason that he determines to have the "grand clear

out" at the Birmingham factory; his avowed motive, to get a
square deal for Tarver, the young designer who sides with
him in the conflict between youth and age, is not realistic.

The complexity lacking in *Blindness* and discovered in *Living* is not due simply to the bald inclusion of the elements
of opposition, it is partly an achievement of the style. The
style of *Blindness* is conventional for its period; that is to
say, it is Georgian;[17] and it is as little functional as a style
may be. Green himself regards it, or at least parts of it,
as an improvement over what he had written two years earlier, comparing, in his autobiography, the two following passages of which the second became part of *Blindness*. The first
passage was written on the back of a photograph.

> I flatter myself that this is not in the least like me: how could it
> be what with the irritation at the photographer and the idiocy of
> being photographed. I resolutely posed myself and looked out with
> an easily recognizable defiance at the paste board I was to mes-
> merize. There is anger and resignation in the futile flabby sneer
> of the lips, there is a terrible lankness, toughness almost in the
> figure. Altogether a horrible photograph.

Then:

> He was alone for the moment. Nan had left him to take a cup of tea.
> The nurse was taking the daily walk that was necessary to her trade
> union health, and Mrs. Haye had gone up to the village to console
> Mrs. Trench, whose week-old baby was dying. Herbert, leaning
> on the sill of the kitchen window, was making noises at Mrs. Lane
> while she toyed with a chopper, just out of his reach. Weston was
> lost in wonder, love and praise before the artichokes, he had a
> camera in his pocket and had taken a record of their splendour.
> Twenty years on and he would be showing it to his grandchildren,
> to prove how things did grow in the old days. Twenty years ago
> Pinch had seen better. Harry was hissing over a sporting paper;
> Doris in an attic was letting down her hair, she was about to plait
> the two soft pigtails. Jenny, the laundry cat, was very near the
> sparrow now, by the bramble in the left-hand corner of the drying-
> ground. [18]

Although he does not say so explicitly, Green evidently considers the second passage superior because it is more objective. The greater objectivity depends not on the fact that the
first passage is about himself and the second about a variety
of objects, but rather on the fact that the second describes

a man's condition in terms of precise percepts of the external world as the first does not. The matters observed have about them a kind of unprogressive regularity or a dull permanence: Mrs. Trench's babies are eternally dying; Herbert, Mrs. Lane, and the others are continually thus fatuously engaged; the cat takes an eternity to spring at the sparrow. The passage is first an objective description of the phenomena which go to make up a certain moment in time: "This is how it was." But then the important function of the phenomena is that they provide a description of the quality of the boy's loneliness; they suggest its tedium by the regularity of their occurrence and its insupportable length by the stretch of forty years between Pinch's potential for looking back and Weston's for looking forward. In another way the percepts by their triviality convey a sense of the great wastage of the faculty of sight.

Proceeding by the controlled description of one thing in terms of another in perfectly defined images, the second passage, which gives "a set of objects which shall be the formula of that *particular* emotion," provides a good, accurate description.

But *Blindness* is not all, not mostly, of this order of accuracy. In many passages there are expressions that deliberately fall short of imagery, or words without unequivocal reference which for the reader must remain only words. The difference is that between two kinds of poets that Stephen Spender has remarked: those who use language as an instrument to get their experiences into words and those who merely manipulate poetic phrases. The following passages, which are more typical of *Blindness*, manifest one of the most disagreeable traits of romantic writing, be it poetry or prose: the impaired definition of images which purveys a vague, unclean excitement.

> It was getting colder; the sun had not been out all day, and one always knew when the sun was out. A blackbird warned as he fled down wind. The *air round was stealthy.*
>
> It was so full of *little hints;* the air carried up little noises and then hurried them away again. . . . The rain had stopped falling now, and he was straining to catch the *slightest secrets that were in the winds.* . . .

When they [the boy and the girl] were there they would talk of
everything, and he would find out her life, why her hand was like
that, and why she *trembled the air in a room*. . . . A wind would
come down to *wreathe rings about them—how lyrical!* But June
would be so charming; she must be, and she had such strong hands.
Besides, her voice was lovely; there was *something wild* in it and
something asleep there as well. . . . But they would go on walking out together like any boy and his slut, and he would explore
in her for the *things* that her voice told him were there, and that
had never been let out. . . .

But then the sun came out. It was changed now. The hut, the trees
and each leaf suddenly had a *spirit* of their own. And the wind bore
them down to you that they might whisper in your ear, and be com-
panions as you sat in the dark. [19]

Here I have italicized those words and phrases that, more
than the others, seem to render the passage ineffective as
descriptive prose. They are insubstantial and vague; they tell
us nothing. To say that "the air round was stealthy" or that
there was "something asleep" in a girl's voice or, even more
absurd, that "she trembled the air in a room" is not to trans-
mit a perception. Such phrases, in fact, prove the uselessness of the style as a means of perception. What they do is
to instruct the reader more or less peremptorily, in a conventional romantic code, to engender in himself an unspecified
excitement.

It may be objected that these passages offer in adolescent
terms the stream of an adolescent consciousness and that
immaturity is naturally apt to dwell upon the insubstantial.
But if we are to take delight in such a marriage between the
point-of-view character and the style, we need a sense of
detachment from him for vantage. And the author offers no
opportunity for gaining such a detachment. Nor is the asper-
ity of these objections and others that follow diminished by
the consideration that the author is partly engaged in trying
to describe what amounts to a new faculty derived from the
intensification of aural and other sensibilities as a compensation for blindness. For the unfamiliar is more often than not
the business of the novel, and the author best presents it in
terms of the familiar.

This proposition seems self-evident. But it may be objected that the following precept of Green's, in *Pack My Bag,*

constitutes a denial of it: "Prose should be a long intimacy between strangers with no direct appeal to what both may have known. "[20] Now this can only be true in a special sense that is not the fundamental one. Fundamentally the very process of communication by language requires mutual agreement as to the denotation of the counters it uses: only by arrangement and rearrangement of the known can the unknown be transmitted. The failure of communication in the passages quoted above is a fundamental one: as to the value of the counters used there is no mutual agreement. The failure is due to a misconception in literary economics, common in the nineteenth century and early twentieth, that more can be got out than was put in. Landor's comment on Wordsworth is to the point: the lover with a lock of his mistress' gold hair, no matter how valuable it may be to *him*, will receive from the jeweler no more than the gold is worth in the common market.

The laboring here of this rather obvious proposition is calculated. For in view of Green's precept and of his later stylistic adventures and achievements, it seems important to emphasize that no advantages accrue to prose from mutual disagreement as to the denotation of its words. The wealth of connotation may, of course, fluctuate. However, nothing but bewilderment comes from blurring the outlines of the fundamental counters of communication.

The failure to achieve objectivity in the quoted passages is an index of the author's failure to achieve detachment. What to the author is gold through affection is nothing to the reader. The author presumably strives for detachment in the fierce "like any boy and his slut, " but this phrase only stands out starkly alone and fails to leaven the rest of the passage. It is beside my purpose to discuss the biographical issue to decide whether Green's involvement may be attributed to his proximity to the material or to his extreme youth as a writer, or both. But what may be empirically observed is that in his second novel, *Living*, Green realized a detachment that appears only sporadically in his first. The important technique by which he achieved detachment is, of course, irony, or rather various ironies which both frame and suffuse the novel. But I wish to consider first a technique of secondary usefulness though unique and immediately remarkable in Green.

The merit of the first of the two quotations from *Blindness* that the second lacks is its clear and precise images. Green communicates the feeling of being alone by *enargia,* the style that exhibits objects vividly, as Shakespeare communicates the feeling of winter in the lyric "When Icicles Hang by the Wall." He has experienced what he describes, both the details in the scene and the loneliness for which the scene is the formula. The difference between the first passage and the second is not the difference between concretion and abstraction but rather between concretion and concretion *manqué*. It may be locked at in another way: the first passage, because it is interested in referents, uses words as vexatious and constricting but unavoidable vehicles to indicate the referents which are the counters of communication. The second, deliberately choosing words whose referents are not only not hard and clear but are shy of coming forth, tends to use the words themselves as counters of communication.

Now the style of *Living,* to speak generally of what is most varied, is at pains to minimize the constriction, which words impose, by sheer economy in use of them. [21] The most readily remarkable feature of this economy is the frequent elimination outside the dialogue of *the,* suggested possibly by the Warwickshire dialect prevalent in Birmingham in which *the* becomes the frequently inaudible apocopate, *t'*. [22] There is a similar economy in the use of the indefinite article, of auxiliary verbs, and of the verb *to be.* Often the words that correctly relate a modifier are omitted, and participles and phrases are left dangling. Relative, possessive, and other pronouns may be omitted, and subordination is thereby impaired. There is a corresponding prodigality in the use of emphatic *that,* in repetition, and in the words *and* and *then.*

In the resulting bald prose the objects presented are more solid while the relationship between them is weakened, as if the author had voluntarily foregone the advantage prose has over painting. [23] A random test of this description of Green's prose against the novel may prove disappointing, for the style is varied and includes passages that show none of the features mentioned. But the general tendency of the style is significant since in preferring the percept to the relationship, the texture to the structure, it approaches the style of Imagist poetry

and more particularly of the dream[24] to which the structure
of certain of the later novels of Green is analogous.

Another important departure from the style of *Blindness*
is the self-conscious and sometimes elaborate use of figurative language in *Living*. The heroic simile of the pigeon, although elaborated with nonessentials after the heroic manner, fits point by point that which it illuminates. It is just:
Johnson would say, "He that never found it wonders how he
missed it." Coleridge would call it a product of the imagination as opposed to one of the fancy. But there are other figures in which the discovery of such easy equivalences is impossible. The following is the most elaborate figure of speech
in the novel.

> Miss Glossop was downcast. We have seen her feeling, when she
> thought of Tom Tyler, had been like a tropical ocean with an in-
> finite variety of colour. As her boat came near dry land you could
> see coral reefs and the seaweed where in and out went bright fishes,
> as her thoughts turned to him so you could see all these in her eyes.
> Further out, in the deep sea, in her deeper feeling about him when
> he was away, now and again dolphins came up to feed on the surface
> of that ocean. And in her passage she disturbed shoals of flying
> fish. These were the orchestration of her feelings, so transparently
> her feeling lapped him and her thoughts, in shoals, fed on the top,
> or hung poised for two moments in the shallows. [25]

Here the dry land stands for Tom, the boat for Hannah,
the ocean for her feelings, and the dolphins for her thoughts.
But the figure is the product of the faculty of fancy, in Coleridge's sense. These equivalences, unlike those in the heroic
simile quoted earlier, are limited; and the limitation is deliberately maintained by the temporary destruction of the allegory—"you could see all these in her eyes"—and by the end
of the passage where, unless we relinquish the equivalences,
thoughts must swim in feelings.

In this figure equivalence is merely a rough and ready, ex-
pendable framework in which the images may be mounted.
There is ironic delight in the usefulness of this framework;
it can even be made to accommodate the flying fish: "These
were the orchestration of her feelings." But the important
counters of communication are the images themselves, the
texture of which, with almost no help from the structural re-

lationship between the two halves of the simile, conveys the excitement and joy of the girl's romantic mental excursion. In other words, unlike the heroic simile where the likeness between Lily's thoughts and the pigeons is itself important, this figure reveals almost nothing by the mere equivalence between Hannah and the boat. What is important is that, this equivalence granted, the mustered percepts of the bright fish, the coral reef, the flying fish, and the rest reveal to us something about the girl, her sensations of delight, by a process akin to *enargia* but more exploratory. [26]

The reliance here upon the image as such and the relatively small use made of relationship are a minor instance of the practice of Green's precept quoted above. The likeness between Hannah and the boat, her feelings and the ocean, and so forth, are of the fancy; the concretes cannot be known in the way that those can that belong to similes coined by the imagination. The pigeon, to return to the Homeric simile, is known fully and immediately to the reader, who is perfectly directed by the structural relationship and can with complete safety enlarge upon whatever details of the bird are given.

The object that is not known at once, however, may in the course of the "long intimacy between strangers" become known. This is the way it is with the image of Siam, which only gradually achieves connotation. The image, or rather the word, as it had better be initially designated, occurs first toward the end of Mr. Bridges' tirade when he finds the men smoking in the lavatory: "'Firm'll be ruined. Debtor prison. Siam. Bankrupt. '"[27] It next occurs when Bridges learns Tarver has called him crazy: "'Crazy am I? You see who'll be in Siam first, him or me. '"[28] It occurs again, this time in quotation marks, in the angry thoughts of Dick Dupret: "We shall be ruined cried he in his mind, business will go bankrupt, 'to Siam, Siam, ' 'Not functioning to its full capacity for production': the old men are smashing it. . . ."[29]

We gradually come to know Siam as connoting for Bridges (when Dick uses the word he is quoting Bridges) the horrors of bankruptcy and madness. With further use, however, the connotation is enlarged. Tom Tyler, Hannah Glossop's playboy beau, is "back from Siam, '"[30] where, we later learn, he is the "unpaid adjunct to British Resident" and pursues the gay life.[31] Siam thus signifies bankruptcy for Tyler too, insofar as he is unpaid, although to him it is an enjoyable state. In this way Siam gradually comes to be known. And then it returns with dramatic irony to its first use to endow the passage with its gathered ironical force. It is a small example of the process Green describes. But it is significant in its relation to the novel as a whole, in that it mirrors the contradictory attitudes of old and young, morbid horror and irresponsible delight, toward the same thing.

The most important departure in the style of *Living* from that of *Blindness*, and one that greatly increases the detachment of the author, is the use of irony. It is irony that distinguishes *Living* as a comic novel. The hero of *Blindness* is not, of course, of tragic stature; but at the same time it is impossible to condescend toward him. He is never shown in the light in which his real-life counterpart must inevitably at some time or another appear: the self-important, desperately protestant introvert, a kind of twentieth-century Shelley. He may never be laughed at. Similarly Entwhistle, though foolish, is not the fool; the reader may blush at his excesses, but he may not smile without destroying the tone of the novel. In *Living*, on the other hand, the irony cuts the characters down to their comic dimensions.

Thus, for blunt example, though he may sympathize with Dick Dupret in his struggles with old men, the reader cannot accord him such support as he gives to John Haye for his exertions, having seen Dupret furtively picking his nose behind a book. Directly compromising aspects of character are infrequently presented, however, and Lily in particular is unscathed by them. There are, on the other hand, general means by which all the characters are trimmed to a stature to which the reader can condescend.

First, the title itself, in suggesting more than is actually depicted, is ironic. The stock response to "living" is heightened living—living as opposed to mere existence. What the novel presents is mere existence, or at best existence touched inconstantly by living. And thus a dull irony suffuses the scenes and activities.

Second, the sharp juxtaposition of upper-class and lower-class living provides reciprocal irony. Thus, for example, if Lily's joy and warmth at walking with Bert in the light of street lamps render specious the drawing-room antics of Tyler and Hannah on the following page, these in their worldly setting render the others primitive and childish.[32] A commentary on the lower classes, and of the same comic order, is made by the dialect they invariably speak. For dialect in English novels, or in England generally, produces comedy far more than in America, where it is less an index of social class.

Then there is the irony produced when an acting agent in one situation becomes acted upon in an analogous one. Thus Craigan and Bridges, each an autocrat in his respective sphere, are acted upon by a higher power more arbitrary than their own. Lily, planning to flee possession by the father, prays for the possession of a child; Lily, again, possessed by Craigan, comes to possess him; Bert Jones, fleeing Bridges, his father substitute, is frustrated in his airy plans by his failure to find his real father. The irony exists in the misconception of all these persons that they are free, autonomous agents. The irony is a little more pointed by the author's regular designation of them as Mr., Mrs., or Miss.

In a study of *Living*, the discovery of substantial images, of ironies, and of similes, both the imaginative with immediate and the fanciful with latent connotations, does not exhaust the topic of the style of this novel. But these are the important techniques because they mark direction. An analysis of an early passage may demonstrate the complexity of Green's style and the kind of expression it achieves partly by means of the techniques described.

Standing in foundry shop son of Mr. Dupret thought in mind and it seemed to him that these iron castings were beautiful and he reached out fingers to them, he touched them; he thought and only in machinery it seemed to him was savagery left now for in the country, in summer, trees were like sheep while here men created what you could touch, wild shapes, soft like silk, which would last and would be working in great factories, they made them with their hands. He felt more certain and he said to himself it was wild incidental beauty in these things where engineers had thought only of the use put to them. He thought, he declaimed to himself this was the life to lead, making useful things which were beautiful, and the gladness to make them, which you could touch; but when he was

most sure he remembered, he remembered it had been said before
and he said to himself, "Ruskin built a road which went nowhere
with the help of undergraduates and in so doing said the last word
on that." And then what had been so plain, stiff and bursting inside him like soda fountains, this died as a small wind goes out,
and he felt embarrassed standing as he did in fine clothes.[33]

First, the paragraph describes a reverie that withdraws
the boy from time and from the place where his incongruity is
manifest in his fine clothes. The passage begins slowly, almost
tentatively, the actions it describes being broken down into
their component parts: twice "he thought and . . . it seemed";
"he reached out fingers . . . he touched." Then, as the boy is
brought with the help of sensuous excitement to that familiar
romantic pitch which enables us to see into the life of things,
the passage rises to a crescendo, and he delivers himself
with some certainty of his great original idea about life. The
lightly ironic fact that he "declaims" this thought makes him
absurd, mocking him slightly, hinting at the orator in him,
deriding his disproportionate solemnity before the small discovered truth. Finally, as he realizes that the idea is not
original and that he has thought out nothing more than what was
a commonplace to Ruskin's old generation, the reverie dies,
and he returns to time and place.

He did not, we observe, immediately handle the castings;
and the hesitancy in the solid image of fingers, not hands,
first reaching out and later touching, conveys a veneration
exaggerated and slightly absurd. Next, the beauty of the castings was inherent in their savagery which surpassed that of
trees. The connotation of "trees," supplied later, shows they
represent the romantic withdrawal of the working class from
the factory and what it stands for. To young Dupret the castings he hardly dares to touch, made with hands here in the
factory, offer a thrill akin to an erotic experience (which for
everyone in the novel connotes withdrawal) in that what has
such potentiality (great factories) is soft and tactile. The beauty of the castings, however, is only partly sensuous. It is
partly dependent upon the state of mind achieved by his imaginative exertion. But when the outcome proves unoriginal
the reverie dissolves, the beauty of the castings is invalidated,
and the embarrassed boy recognizes his absurdity.

The paragraph describes the kind of romantic excursion away from reality found elsewhere in the novel. Its general enveloping irony consists in the fact that the upper class may discover romance and withdrawal where the lower finds only harsh reality, that iron castings are objects of romantic beauty only to the observer who enjoys the kind of detachment from them for which fine clothes are a label.

It is readily admitted that the paragraph cited is not picked at random and that the active operation of the style is intermittent throughout the novel. Further, where the style is operative it is conspicuously self-conscious and unmodish. Nevertheless, even the occasional employment of a style that is functional rather than what in *Blindness* tended to be a mere romantic matrix purveying a dull emotion from the outside marks a significant advance.

And the advance in style is in turn an index of the better perception manifest in *Living*. For the style that minimizes the opacity that words must offer and tries to reproduce the solidity of the referent itself is a better instrument for the perception of reality than that which, dealing in vague referents, prefers a sterile trafficking with the words themselves. Meanwhile the career of Lily, in which dreams are translated into the terms of necessity, is the predicate of a closer perception of human affairs than that which formulates the career of John Haye, for whom dreams come true. And with this closer perception in *Living*, the new departure of style in the novel is perfectly consonant.

4. PARTY GOING

The phenomenon of human development described with increasing complexity in *Blindness* and *Living* is further explored in *Party Going* under the likely metaphor of traveling. The destination of the party is the south of France; and since all of them except Angela have been there before, it objectifies that sunny utopia familiar in dream content and essentially a thing remembered. The utopian quest is specifically the business of Max Adey's party only; the other people on the station platform are merely acting out a routine in limbo; "it was the end of a day for them, the beginning of time for our party."[1]

In none of "our" characters, however, is the desire to travel absolute. Each of them is beset by his own private anxiety or guilt, or both, which becomes a deterrent from traveling and a reason and excuse for retreat. Max, for example, is thwarted by his feelings of guilt. Growth for him, as we shall see, consists in his diverting his sexual quest away from Amabel and directing it toward Julia. Amabel is known the length of England for her conventional beauty; she belongs to the same social class as Max; and their purchasing power runs to the same fashionable interior decorations. Hence, when his own departure threatens to disrupt his relationship with her and to disturb the stasis she represents, his guilt feelings are aroused. Later, as a result of her impact on him when she arrives at the hotel, he persuades himself that he does not wish to travel. Similarly, guilt and anxiety with reference to Auntie May inhibit Claire, extend to Evelyna, and involve

40

Julia. Evelyna and Claire conspire with each other concerning
Aunt Julia's illness. Angela nourishes intermittent guilt feelings toward Robin and cannot make up her mind whether she
wants him to leave her or not. And Julia, chronically anxious
about her charms—a little wooden pistol, an egg with ivory ele-
phants in it, and a top—and having already returned home once
to look for them, tries persistently to keep in touch with her
chauffeur and thereby to leave open the chance of returning to
the comfort of home. Alex overtly advises return.

The deterrent common to all the party is the fog and darkness. The condition for self-creation is a temporary withdrawal
from the self-in-the-world which, as seen in *Blindness* and, in
fact, regularly in Green and frequently in other authors, is figured as a withdrawal from light into darkness. However, Green
uses this withdrawal in his own way and for his own purposes.
Certain of his novels, including *Party Going,* play extensive
variations upon this theme of darkness. But I wish here to
quote a short passage from his "Mr. Jonas, " a short story
written about the same time as *Caught,* which, using abstract
terms and an alternative metaphor, forms a concise and useful comment upon the metaphoric value of darkness.

> Accustomed, as all were, to sights of this kind [hoses playing on
> a burning building], there was not one amongst us who did not now
> feel withdrawn into himself, as though he had come upon a place
> foreign to him but which he was aware he had to visit, as if it were
> a region the conditions in which he knew would be something be-
> tween living and dying, not, that is, a web of dreams, but rather
> such a frontier of hopes or mostly fears as it may be in the destiny
> of each, or almost all, to find, betwixt coma and the giving up of
> living. [2]

The description of Julia's first descent into the darkness
may well be cited here; it shows her accepting certain of the
terms of self-creation enumerated above: loss of identity,
guilt, and alienation.

> As she stepped out into this darkness of fog above and left warm
> rooms with bells and servants and her uncle who was one of Mr.
> Roberts' directors—a rich important man—she lost her name and
> was all at once anonymous; if it had not been for her rich coat she
> might have been any typist making her way home.
> Or she might have been a poisoner, anything. Few people passed

her and they did not look up, as if they also were guilty. As each
and everyone went about their business they were divided by this
gloom and were nervous. . . . [3]

Further withdrawal into darkness is effected by the party
when, divested of all their worldly luggage, they enter the
hotel. Julia thought "it was like an enormous doctor's waiting
room and that it would be like that when they were all dead
and waiting at the gates. "[4]

The hotel and some of the human beings associated with it
bear striking if accidental resemblance to Kafka: the man
with the glass eye trying unsuccessfully to light his cigar has
no specific associations; the clownish young men on the window
ledges outside mouthing obscenities at the old lady within recall
the assistants locked out of the schoolhouse in *The Castle;*
the maidservant leaning out of the window to be grabbed at by
the man outside is reminiscent of maidservants in Kafka who
are so frequently the victims of arbitrary cruelty. The hotel
itself, in the difficulty with which it is entered or left, calls
to mind Kafka's castle; but this is no more than a mere resemblance, for the castle represents a destination and the hotel
only a stage in the journey.

The essential nature of the hotel may be illuminated, however, by comparison with prison, pit, cave, or with whatever replaces, in contemporary literature, the older image
of water as the local embodiment of the archetypal dark womb
from which new life emerges. There is, for example, the
dungeon that Jeremiah Beaumont willingly enters in *World
Enough and Time,* in which the darkness is pregnant with
life, reminding Beaumont of a cave he had once crawled into
where it seemed as though "the dark were about to pulse. "[5]
Or there is the pit where Thomas Mann's Joseph is confined;
or the cave in which Pietro Spina, of *The Seed beneath the
Snow,* takes refuge. He describes to his grandmother the
darkness and the filth. "But I must tell you one thing, " he
adds,

as soon as my eyes became accustomed to the semi-darkness and
I began to distinguish its contents . . . an indescribable feeling of
serenity and repose came over me, a deep sense of peace such as
I had never known in all my life before, which relieved me of all

my worries. Grandmother, my presence in that place seemed the
most natural thing in the world. "Here I have come to rest, *'Inveni
portum,'"* I thought; this was the end of my long pilgrimage, the
supreme reality, stripped of illusory consolations, that I had been
seeking. [6]

There is the prison in which Meursault, in *The Stranger,* is
incarcerated. After his struggle with the chaplain, Meursault
sleeps.

> Then, just on the edge of daybreak, I heard a steamer's siren.
> People were starting on a voyage to a world which had ceased to
> concern me forever. Almost for the first time in many months I
> thought of my mother. . . . With death so near, Mother must have
> felt like someone on the brink of freedom, ready to start life all
> over again. [7]

Each of these largely analogous situations has, of course, its
own peculiarities. Meursault's condition is doubly relevant to
our immediate interests in that his superb peace of mind was
not gratuitously given to him but was a state he had attained
after a period of tormented, inactive waiting.

Now, the onerous burden of waiting in the darkness is frequently inflicted also upon Green's characters, who for the
most part are incapable of stillness. The first chapter of the
third part of *Blindness* is entitled "Waiting"; but John Haye
passes through the period scarcely ruffled. Waiting preys on
characters elsewhere;[8] it preys least on those who can escape
it, at least temporarily, by taking some relevant action in connection with immediate concerns. Mrs. Dupret, in *Living,* is
doubly victimized when, waiting for her husband to die, she
is deprived, by his partial recovery, of the demands for physical effort that had mitigated the distress of waiting. Her departure from his sickbed and her re-entry into London life, though
criticized by her guests, are her proper response to her trials.
The characters in *Party Going* waiting in the hotel are generally
prevented from taking any action about anything. Alex and Robert are sent on manifold errands, but since they are virtually
unable to leave the hotel they accomplish nothing satisfying.
For the same reason, nothing practical can be done about Auntie May, although there is considerable bustle on her behalf.

Around such situations in Green where activity is precluded,

a tense atmosphere develops; men and women are obsessed by
groundless fears, and what is insignificant assumes grotesque
importance. Hence, in *Party Going,* the man who, out of a
camaraderie otherwise foreign to the novel, follows Auntie
May after her removal to the hotel, becomes an object of un-
reasoning fear; the question whether Embassy Richard did or
did not write the letter becomes absurdly intense; and confess-
edly irrational fear centers on Auntie May's dead pigeon.

The people both outside and inside the hotel manifest alienation one from another. Outside, although everyone is singing,
"soon they did not agree about songs"; then "no one sang at
all" and "desolation overtook them. "[9] Desolation, only less
naked, also overtakes those inside: two or more of them are
continually conspiring to exclude one or more of the others.
They are sharply divided about Embassy Richard and about
the identity of the "hotel detective. " Angela feels that all of
them "even the nannies are in league to make one feel out
of it"[10] and proceeds to contrive to make Robin feel out of it.
Julia, who has thought of no one but herself, feels they are
all selfish.

The dreary situation within the hotel is not in the end left
entirely unresolved. It is doubtful whether the advent of Embassy Richard and the final settlement of the question of the
letter go far to defeat the alienation that the problem had thrown
into relief. But his presence and the tacit understanding that
he will squire Amabel undeniably advance Max's affairs. Moreover, at the end, the train is announced and, although the
difficulties of getting the party and its baggage together seem
almost insuperable, it is reasonable to suppose that they will
eventually board it.

The darkness of the hotel is not absolute darkness, "cleansing affection from the temporal" and, more important, depriving of personality those characters who are striving for
growth. Indeed, their personality is only too evident. There
is, however, another means than darkness by which personality may be submerged. It is apparent that the utopia for
which the travelers are bound, as already remarked in Max's
case, has the traditional connotation of the perfect sexual
encounter. In Amabel's vision the sexual content of the destina-

tion is clear; "into that smiling country their journey together would open in their hearts as she hoped, the promised land. "[11] In Julia's it is confined to the overtones of "blushes" and possibly of "fainting": "But when it was fine and you sat on the terrace for dinner looking over a sea of milk with a sky fainting into dusk with the most delicate blushes—Oh! she cried in her heart, if only we could be there now. "[12] The same utopia "lay back of all their minds or feelings, " and it connoted, for the women among them, the possession of Max, if not to the extent of marriage at least so far as to be able to control his drinking.

Many of the apparently incongruous and unexplained fears of the party, therefore, may be read as fears for the failure of sexual opportunity or adequacy. The hotel detective, for example, is familiar in anecdote as the inhibitor of sexual affairs. The dead pigeon, the dark fear for Claire and Evelyna, may be read for them (but not for Auntie May) as their physical or circumstantial impotence. Julia is concerned about her charms, which are her sexual charms, and about keeping them hidden, a secrecy she will allow to be violated only under the right conditions.

The sexual encounter is no mere animal comfort for the party as it is for Thomson, Julia's chauffeur, who seems to regard it as an alternative to tea. [13] It is, or may be, a significant part of the process of self-creation. Sexuality provides a means of both asserting selfhood and at the same time breaking out of alienation. When mutual, it is a sharing, which reconciles the opposites: maximal selfishness in taking and maximal generosity in giving. The question of sex in *Party Going* most concerns Max, for whom two kinds of sexual relationships are submitted as possibilities. There is the improper sexuality offered by Amabel, who, revealed as utterly narcissistic during the scene in the bathroom, willing to take but not give, offers only annihilation of the self-creating ego. Her unwillingness to appear naked even before her lovers is indicative of her sexual role in which she is to be entirely subject and never object. "If we start with the first revelation of the Other as a look, " says Sartre,

we must recognize that we experience our inapprehensible being-for-others in the form of a *possession*. I am possessed by the

Other; the Other's look fashions my body in its nakedness, causes
it to be born, sculptures it, produces it as it *is*, sees it as I shall
never see it. The Other holds a secret—the secret of what I am. He
makes me be and thereby he possesses me, and this possession is
nothing other than the consciousness of possessing me. [14]

Amabel utterly avoids the possession of herself. But sex with
her, while it spells annihilation of self, offers also comfortable, conventional security toward which, in the face of the
terrors of the unknown, Max is tempted to regress.

He walked round and round where she was sitting as though she
were a river and a bridge off which he felt impelled to jump to
drown. . . .
   He stood in front of her and she fixed him with her eyes which
drew him like the glint a hundred feet beneath and called on him
to throw himself over. [15]

Then there is the proper sexuality Julia offers Max which
is a unique and not conventional experience, for she is a virgin.
And it is a mutual giving and taking:

And as she hoped this party would be, if she could get a hold of Max,
it would be as though she could take him back into her life from
where it had started and show it to him for them to *share* in a much
more exciting thing of their own, artichokes, pigeons and all, she
thought and laughed aloud. [16]

What no doubt harasses the reader most in this novel and
what harasses Claire and Evelyna too is the mystery of Auntie
May's dead pigeon. The "meaning" of this episode is not absolutely clear. Walter Allen says it "cannot be paraphrased";[17]
and that statement is as true for this poetic device as it is
for any other. But although the meaning cannot be paraphrased,
some light may be thrown upon the episode by a gathering of
"the web of insinuations" and a consideration of its relationship to the novel. The main business of the novel is the "departure" of young people for maturity. In a word, it concerns
the death of youth, the abstract, which formerly had been
presided over by the nannies and Miss Fellowes. Miss Fellowes now sees fit to watch over the death of youth and to grant
it a decent burial. Her care of the pigeon figures her last
proper function as a guardian of youth. But if she had finally
disposed of it her usefulness would be at an end. She would

be cast off, like nannies elsewhere in Green when their matur-
ing protégés pass beyond their control. Naturally she seeks
to protract her usefulness; hence she clings to the bird, cling-
ing thereby to life itself.

The pigeon, however, is only a local figure in a novel of
which the large figurative structure now needs consideration.
A description of growth, when it is the inward thing and not
merely physical waxing, demands the use of metaphor for
its expression. Metaphor, in fact, is even necessary for its
designation: "growth." The metaphor by nature must take
the form of outward actions or circumstances. Meanwhile
there are outward actions and circumstances that are literal
but that, being subtended by inward postures, are inevitably
of the same order as the metaphorical. In literature concerned
with growth, therefore, there is an unavoidable arbitrariness
in distinguishing between figure and literal fact, or there is at
least arbitrariness in disposing the emphasis. To what extent, we may ask, is "I have put away childish things" figurative and to what extent factual?

The point, it will be objected, is purely academic: inward
actions, since they are not *actions,* offer no drama. The drama
must by nature exist only in the outward actions which demand
most of our interest. And it will also be argued that the modern
reader is inclined anyway to understand that actions result
from inward promptings. But the point ceases to be academic
when, by emphasis given to what on its own outward account
is small, or by any sufficiently severe violation of outward
proportion, as occurs in *Party Going* and some later novels,
the reader is virtually sent elsewhere for a rationale.

I have considered John Haye's blindness as essentially literal, [18] albeit accompanied by a supplementary psychological
rationale, for the emphasis is so laid by the author. To the
question, Why was he blind? a material answer will suffice:
He was struck by flying glass. (There is, of course, the hint
that the affliction had an inward cause.) Similarly, if it is asked
with reference to *Living,* Why did Lily leave home? the answer
may be given strictly in terms of the outward manifestations
of the novel. But, to come to *Party Going,* where there are
emphases for which an outward rationale does not account,
if it is asked, Why did the party enter the hotel? the first

answer, Because it was comfortable, must be supplemented
by the second, Because the hotel is a metaphor for the stage
of withdrawal from the world in the process of growth. [19] And
between these two answers there is a great difference in dimension.

The difference between *Party Going*, however, and the earlier two novels is not, of course, absolute in this respect.
Far from it: "When the poet's mind is perfectly equipped for
work, it is constantly amalgamating disparate experience."
It is no more possible for the author to isolate the external
from the internal than for the schizophrenic to separate empirical knowledge from his obsessing fear. The mind, like
Green's pigeons in *Living*, continually returns.

In *Party Going* the author chooses the metaphor of traveling
to describe growth. This is the kind of likely metaphor that
"upon its first production [is] acknowledged to be just"; "he
that never found it wonders how he missed it, " and repeated
usage endows it with respectability. It is like Pope's comparison of a student's progress to an Alpine journey, which Johnson
found so excellent in "An Essay on Criticism": the elements
inherent in one situation whether designated or not may find
equivalents in the other; and the equivalence is infinitely extensible. Such a figure is that of the shooting star that Coleridge uses to illustrate the function of the imagination. Such a
figure is darkness, the metaphor derived ultimately from Neo-
Platonic thought, which represents the withdrawal of the self-
in-the-world.

Such natural figures as are produced by the imagination,
however, although their cross equivalence may be infinitely extensible, do not portray the totality of the abstract. [20] That is to
say, if one facet of growth is likened to traveling, the metaphor
of the imagination can show how very like traveling that facet is
but it cannot educe whatever other facets growth may have. The
metaphor of the imagination is useful when what is known is to
be illuminated or limned out in communication. It is, perhaps,
to hint at a matter discussed below, a figure that belongs to an
age of good manners (in I. A. Richards' sense) in literature,
when known truths are to be consolidated.

The operation of the fancy Coleridge regarded as inferior

to that of the imagination; it worked with "fixities and def-
inites" that did not submit themselves to the "esemplastic"
power; "Milton had a *highly imaginative,* Cowley a *very fanciful* mind. "[21] Nevertheless, the figure formed by the fancy
rather than by the imagination is the proper figure for exploring the possibilities of the nature of an abstract. Fancy,
not imagination, is the active, searching faculty. The assign-
ment of the term by Ludovicus Vives, who is given a hearing
in Coleridge, is of interest: *"Phantasia* . . . is employed by
Vives to express the mental power of comprehension, or the
active function of the mind; and *imaginatio* for the receptivity
(vis receptiva) of impressions, or for the *passive* perception. "[22]

Hence, for example, Donne habitually "builds in the mode of
fancy" as proper for active exploration. According to William
Empson, he could write on occasion "without realizing quite
how much . . . he was getting into his language";[23] which is
to say, working at it another way, he does not know how far
language will discover the topic. Similarly the figures of other
poets of the Renaissance or of the twentieth century may be
regarded as forays into heterogeneous territory, from which
the poet may return empty-handed, with something so far-
fetched it was *not* "worth the carriage, " with a "monstrous
image blindly/ Magnified out of praise, " or, more fortunately,
with an image that discovers, with some partial success that
is not to be finally measured, hitherto unknown aspects of his
abstract.

Before discussing the major fanciful metaphor of *Party
Going,* I would note two passages where fanciful metaphors
are being more or less overtly tried out. The first, a failure,
is ludicrous.

Whoever he might be such treatment was bad for him. Max was not
what he had been. . . . It was not Amabel's fault, she was all right
even if she did use him, it was these desperate inexperienced
bitches, he thought, who never banded together but fought everyone
and themselves and were like camels, they could go on for days
without one sup of encouragement. Under their humps they had
tanks of self-confidence so that they could cross any desert area of
arid prickly pear without one compliment, or dewdrop as they

called it in his family, to uphold them. So bad for the desert, he said to himself, developing his argument and this made him laugh aloud. [24]

"Camels" as a pejorative term for women is sufficiently familiar. Alex playfully proceeds to put the metaphor to exploratory use: "camels" by association suggest "desert"; and Alex, not really knowing how this can be made to fit his scheme, makes Max its *significatio* or meaning; this is absurd, and Alex, having discovered nothing, concludes where he started; it is so bad for Max.

The second passage is more interesting.

So crowded together they were . . . so desolate and cold it silenced them. Then one section had begun to chant "we want our train" over and over. . . . And so, having tried everything, desolation overtook them. They were like ruins in the wet, places that is where life has been, palaces, abbeys, cathedrals, throne rooms, pantries, cast aside and tumbled down with no immediate life and with what used to be in them lost rather than hidden now the roof has fallen in. Ruins that is not of their suburban homes for they had hearts, and feelings to dream, and hearts to make up what they did not like into other things. But ruins, for life in such circumstances was only possible because it would not last, only endurable because it had broken down and as it lasted and became more desolate and wet so, as it seemed more likely to be permanent, at least for an evening, they grew restive. Where ruins lie, masses of stone grown over with ivy unidentifiable with the mortar fallen away so that stone lies on stone loose and propped up or crumbling down in mass then as a wind starts up at dusk and stirs the ivy leaves and rain follows slanting down, so deserted no living thing seeks what little shelter there may be, it is all brought so low, then movements of impatience began to flow across all these people and as ivy leaves turn one way in the wind they themselves surged a little here and there in their blind search behind bowler hats and hats for trains. [25]

The key word in this passage is "desolate." By no great leap of association, but with no aid of logic, "desolate" suggests "ruins." Then, if we may sketch crudely the creative process at this point, the author decides to experiment to see whether the likeness between people and ruins, manifest so far only at one point, the common desolation, may be made to reveal something more.

It seems to me that it does reveal something more. But the

yield lends itself reluctantly to accounting. The only complete
answer to the question, How does the image explore the nature
of the people? is the full experience that the whole quotation
above offers its most sensitive reader. The simile, however,
is worth citing as a small and excellent example of the fancy
at work. What it demonstrates well is the "fixity" of both sides
of the simile: ruins remain ruins and people, people. The dis-
parateness of the two is, of course, compromised: we have,
after all, a simile: "They were like ruins." But the extent
to which cross equivalences may be made is entirely within
the author's control. And in order to perform its proper function of exploring, the image of fancy must hold itself aloof.
It must maintain itself rather in the way of Arnold's critic,
standing aside to comment, and must resist all "esemplastic"
efforts to lick it into a shape other than its own or with Pro-
crustean obduracy to equate it with the object it is searching
out. In sharp contrast to this demeanor is that of Arnold's
sea which *becomes* a sea of faith and loses its integrity. It
may be objected that Arnold is comparing an abstract with
a concrete and that the problem is a different one. But then
Green is comparing with ruins the inwardness of the people
and this is also abstract. The important point is that Arnold's
sea has developed properties and activities unknown to marine
observation.

There is a similar tendency in the metaphor of traveling in
Party Going: the journey to the south of France tends to lose
its real nature in accommodating itself to its archetypal function. But, to come to the important fanciful metaphor of the
hotel, this image preserves itself; its naturalistic characteristics are not impaired or clipped away at the edges to enable
it to be forced into a required mold.

The foyer of the hotel and the people in it are described
through the eyes of Julia, whose vision is singularly like Kafka's.

She was in a long hall with hidden lighting and, for ornament, a
vast chandelier with thousands of glass drops and rather dirty. It
was full of people and those who had found seats, which were all
of them too low, lay with blank faces as if exhausted and, if there
was anything to hope for, as though they had lost hope. Most of

them were enormously fat. One man there had a cigar in his mouth, and then she saw he had one glass eye, and in his hand he had a box of matches which now and again he would bring up to his cigar. Just as he was about to strike his match he looked round each time and let his hands drop back to his lap, his match not lighted. Those standing in groups talked low and were rather bent and there was a huge illuminated clock they all kept looking at. Almost every woman was having tea as if she owned the whole tray of it. Almost every man had a dispatch case filled with daily newspapers. She thought it was like an enormous doctor's waiting room and that it would be like that when they were all dead and waiting at the gates. [26]

Here the image may be seen discovering aspects of the abstract by means of its own peculiar embodiments in a manner of which the natural metaphor of darkness or other nonconcrete metaphors are incapable. Something new is learned about the idea of waiting hopelessly, deprived of the possibility of action, in the local setting; the man in the too-low seat, lying back in the posture of a patient, who cannot or perhaps dares not light his cigar. The image purveys not only knowledge but feeling: there is horror in it, or from it, that is not to be derived, for instance, from Eliot's "I said to my soul be still, and wait without hope." The image remains purely naturalistic. Equally naturalistic is the image of "those standing in groups," manifesting fear, like Coleridge's mariners who "listened and looked sideways up." Finally, the image of the women having tea presents vividly the idea of people alienated from each other, hugging to themselves whatever of comfort they can, pretending to possess what they do not possess.

This comment upon the quoted passage is an attempt to trace in a rudimentary fashion the process of exploration. But, brief as it is, it is made reluctantly; for the very act of assigning equivalents or near equivalents to the phenomena in the hotel defeats the proper purpose of that metaphor. The hotel is not simply the image of the archetype (as if that *were* simple!); it is the image that explores it. "If I had known who Godot was," Samuel Becket is reported to have said, "I would have told you." And furthermore the phenomena of the hotel are, for each individual of the party, individual experiences, such unsharable nightmares as exist only in their own terms.

The hotel, like the ruins, maintains its autonomy. Between the image and the *significatio* to which it is yoked by likeness at a point or points, there is no compelling logical relationship, hence no mutilation. This absence of logical relationship, more noticeable in the passage about the ruins where the *significatio* is named, may be noted in little stylistic touches throughout the novel. In the following, for instance, two disparate facts are linked, not as a figure of speech but by their inclusion in a compound sentence. The likeness at one point that brings them together, which is only implied, is their common triviality. "Already both [Claire and Evelyna) had been made to regret they had left such and such a dress behind and it was because he felt it impossible to leave things as they were with Angela . . . that Robin came back to apologize."[27] The absence of logical relationship where it is expected is pervasive. Look at the following two sentences, for example: *and* substitutes for *which* in "She bent down and took a wing then entered a tunnel in front of her, *and* this had DE-PARTURES lit up over it, carrying her dead pigeon";[28] *and* takes the place of *for* in "'Funny thing,' Mr. Adams said *and* he had not listened."[29] There is also at least one place, too long to quote, where *so* introduces a *non sequitur*.

The use of the metaphor of fancy, though not, of course, exclusive of other figures, is a further step in the direction the style began to take between *Blindness* and *Living*. That direction was marked by the replacement of vague insubstantialities or merely words by the reproduction of clear perceptions which seem the more substantial on account of the economy of language. Here the integrity of those percepts is guarded while they are used as metaphors to explore aspects of growth.

In this novel, sexuality as a means either of self-creation or of regression makes its most important appearance. Certainly in later novels it becomes a synecdoche for growth; but here in *Party Going* are presented the alternative terms according to which sexuality may be the means of either the actualization of selfhood or the destruction of it. The candidate for self-creation must enter into only such sexuality as will not compromise his selfhood; confronted by a person

like Amabel, who would put him to a use essentially alien
to his own interests, he must guard his integrity.

Finally, two interesting foreshadowings may be discerned
in *Party Going*. First, the concern with human integrity in
the content is carried over into the technique as the strict
care given the integrity of an image as it enters into union,
as a metaphor or simile, for a purpose alien to its own interests. And this parallelism anticipates a similar one in *Concluding*, where the characters' desire for freedom is mir-
rored by the strategy of the novel. Then the absence of logic
in *Party Going* or the open defiance of it, along with the use
of a figure of speech for large structure, is reminiscent of
the dream. And the author's use of dream technique is clearly
manifest in *Caught*, which will be considered in the next chapter.

5. CAUGHT

The group in *Party Going*, in spite of their dread, are generally oriented toward the future. It is true that Julia returns
to her home in the early stages, and later, by maintaining
contact with her chauffeur, keeps open the avenue of retreat,
and that Max fondly contemplates self-destruction by means
of Amabel. It is true also that there is a general hankering to
turn back. But most of the characters most of the time look
forward, prepared to actualize their freedom despite the pain:
at one level of interpretation, some of them are planning sexual adventures, at another they have all brought luggage and
intend to travel; and there are nannies and an aunt and a boy
friend, all of the past, to wave good-bye to.

In the novels so far considered, the determination to move
forward despite obstacles, manifest in general by Max Adey's
party, has been an attribute of the characters whom Henry
Green admires; and it may be described without reservation
as healthy.[1] While it is good to move ahead, however, there
is posited in Green a proper management of the ideal past away
from which the healthy individual is moving: this past is neither
to be forgotten entirely nor kept in its pristine state; it is to
be integrated with the real future with whatever compromise
may be required. We have already seen Lily, in *Living*, submitting her dreams to such constriction; so Julia, in *Party
Going*, proposes to replace the childhood ideal of virginity,
the secret charm among the bamboos, with the mature ideal
of virginity compromised (but not in the pejorative sense)
or shared in the south of France whither they are all bound.

55

Richard Roe, in *Caught*, on the other hand, desires to forget his childhood and cannot. No adequate reason for his attitude is discoverable; in the following passage where it is described, the prose veers off tangentially, deliberately concealing the reason from the reader and perhaps also from the consciousness of the mind that is being partially revealed.

> Roe had been brought up in this house, among these gardens. The lawns, and most of the undergrowth in the wild garden, the trees, the beds of reed around the moat, all these had become a part of his youth. They had not altered in the twenty years he was growing up. It was he who had changed, who dreaded now, with a hemlock loss of will, to evoke how once he shared these scenes with no one, for he had played alone, who had then no inkling of the insecurity the war would put him in, and who found, when confronted by each turning of a path he knew by heart but which he could never call to mind when he closed his eyes, that the presence, the disclosure again of so much that had not changed and shewed no immediate signs of changing, bore him down back to the state he wished to forget, when he was his son's age and had no more than a son's responsibility to a father.[2]

Childhood also appears under the metaphor of "heraldic cattle" at which Roe and his son, Christopher, throw sticks "to see who could sent these amongst the deer that moved off faster than they came up,"[3] and it is objectified in particular by Christopher himself, in whose presence Roe, initially at least, is uneasy. But although he tries to reject his boyhood garden and is ill at ease with Christopher, he also apparently daydreams about the garden and sentimentalizes his son; and some progress is marked at the end of the book by his ceasing to do so.[4]

Superimposed upon the garden of childhood is the garden that appears in various places in literature as an embodiment of the perfect sexual encounter. The garden in *Caught* is the April garden that we find in various versions of Eden, in the Golden Age, and in the *Roman de la Rose*. It has the traditional appeal of the place looked back to through the selective lens of memory: it is pure and it provides an incredibly beautiful refuge from the squalor, the uncertainty, and the guilt of cur-

rent living. The following passage describes an afternoon
in July that Roe always recalls as April.

> The afternoon, it had been before tea, was hot, swallows darted
> low at the level of her thighs, a blackbird, against three blooms
> bent to the height of its yellow beak, seemed enchanted by terror
> into immobility as the two of them halted, brought to a full stop at
> the corner round which this impermanence caught them fast. He
> turned to her and she seemed his in her white clothes, with a cry
> the blackbird had flown and in her eyes as, speechless, she turned,
> still a stranger, to look into him, he thought he saw the hot, lazy,
> luxuriance of a rose, the heavy, weightless, luxuriance of a rose,
> the curling disclosure of the heart of a rose that, as for a hornet,
> was his for its honey, for the asking, open for him to pierce inside,
> this heavy, creamy, girl turned woman. . . .
> Roses had come above her bare knees under the fluted skirt she
> wore, and the swallows flying so low made her, in his recollec-
> tion, much taller than she had ever been. [5]

It will be observed of this obviously edited memory, first,
that Roe does not wish to obliterate it; rather he nurses it
preciously, partly on account of human nostalgia for the tender
thing lost, but then more significantly because only natures
lower than the human enjoy complete metamorphosis, whereas
the past of a whole man is ineluctably a part of his present
self. Second, it will be observed that the objects of the memory
are bathed in a special light—rather like the vision obtained
through mescalin—and that what is presented is not the thing
as in itself it actually is, or was, but a stylized picture of it.
Again, in a passage which is part of the same memory, there
is a strong suggestion that the color derives not from nature
but from the painter's technique: "Her bare legs had been
the colour of the white roses about them, the red toenails,
through her sandals, stood out against fallen rose leaves of
a red that clashed with the enamel she used, the brick paths
had been fresh, not stained, as the walls here, by soot-saturated rain."[6] There were similar pictures in *Blindness* in the
first period of John Haye's affliction when his memory edited
the past. But here in *Caught* is the first important appearance
of a kind of scene which continually recurs in Green. All such
pictures in the novels are more or less artificial representa-

tions of scenes containing persons or objects that are loved
by one character or possibly more. Further, the scene often
represents a moment of existential community—an ecstasy
which has been or is about to be lost and which, on account
of its dreamlike, unworldly intensity, the character who enjoyed it can never hope to experience again. For such a character the lovely thing remains a spellbinding memory. But
for his present use in advancing his freedom it is impotent.
"Where beauty claims the right to rule," says Kierkegaard,
where for "beauty" we may read "the picture," "it brings
about a synthesis from which spirit is excluded."[7]

For such characters growth consists first in turning deliberately away from the ecstasy, leaving the light for the darkness, the metaphor which appears in *Blindness*. They are attended, of course, by dread and a kind of guilt which, if things
turn out all right in the end, may be compared with the *felix
culpa* of Adam. Second, growth consists not only in not forget-
ting the ecstasy but in bringing it down from its museum ped-
estal where it was dead, and forcing it into dynamic terms
with the workaday world, marrying the existential to the actual.

These two phases of growth are manifested in *Living* where
Lily's dreams, after the period of darkness, are integrated in
imperfect form with the life of necessity. There is in Green's
novels a pattern, uncertainly adhered to, of thesis, antithesis,
synthesis.

For Roe, to return to his specific case, growth consists
in re-enacting the perfect sexual encounter of the innocent
garden, "where brick paths had been fresh, not stained,"
in the world of experience, where the walls were blackened
by "soot-saturated rain."

The darkness into which he descends is that of the blackout
at night, sandbagged windows during the day, in fact the large
and general darkness of the war, which is the major impression the reader retains of the novel. The concomitants of
growth, such as were noted in earlier novels, are to be found
in *Caught* in suitable embodiments provided largely by the
war. The burden of inactive waiting is provided by the period
of the "phony" war, especially in the reiterated concern for
how it will be when the raids start. The war also vicariously
provides figures embodying alienation. In fact, alienation

could find no more definitive image than that of Ilse, a Swedish
girl in London, who is discovered lying naked on a bed in an
unlit flat in the nasty, murky hour before blackout in the winter
of 1940, waiting disconsolately for her brutish lover. Roe's
dread, which accompanies his growth, may not be described
until his peculiar relationship to the percepts in the novel is
clarified. Meanwhile the process of growth itself may be observed.

Roe's first sexual excursion is a failure. At his first meeting
with Prudence and Ilse he is impressed with their icy sterility.
And he himself is alienated from himself, "shut-up" in the uniform, and circumstantially impotent. Prudence's skin "where
neck joined shoulder, covered by small colourless hairs, was
cool to his eyes, like an unwet cake of soap. It was hot. She
had run out in a frock. He was suddenly aware of his tunic,
proofed against flame and water, heavy."

The other girl's skirt is translucent. They live in a white
room with a cactus painted white, and daffodils, made from
sardine tins, and sterile.

> He felt his hands, which were gorged with blood, swollen with
> work. He made out to himself they had grown enormous, that the
> fingers hung at the thighs like strings of raw pork faggots, filthy
> as he was who had not been able to change his heavy sweat-charged
> clothes. For the first time he was conscious that he must smell
> bad while these girls were like bird's feathers, cool and settled.
> . . . Ilse brought him cointreau with water in a long glass and a
> cube of ice. [8]

Neither of these girls can be the means by which the early perfect love may be enacted. Prudence is "knife sharp compared
to the opulence his darling had carried about in her skin."

For Prudence love means a superficial excitement. For
Hilly, on the other hand, to whom Roe turns subsequently,
love is a deeper experience. Furthermore, Hilly's sensations,
and those of Roe himself when he is with her, are sensations
of the garden and are described in garden and rustic images.
Some of these appear in the following, where the word "shared"
is also significant.

> She had been wafted off, was enchanted not entirely by all she had
> had to drink and which was released inside her in a glow of earth

chilled above a river at the noisy night harvest of vines, not altogether by this music, which, literally, was her honey, her feeling's tongue, but as much by sweet comfort, and the compulsion
she felt here to gentleness that was put on her by these couples,
by the blues, by wine, and now by this murmuring, night haunted,
softness shared. [9]

Again, when he kisses her, the sensation is in garden terms:
her "lips' answer, he felt, was of opened figs, wet at dead
of night in a hothouse. "[10] Hilly comes to be the realistic sur-
rogate of Roe's dead wife. And with Hilly, Roe comes to enjoy
an existential experience of which the description, like that
of the original experience, has the special lighting and the
stylized features of a picture.

They lay now on a sofa, naked, a pleasant brutal *picture* by the
light of his coal fire from which rose petals showered on them
as the flames played, deepening the flush spread over contented
bodies. She wriggled over on top, held his dark face and drank it
with her eyes. She had never been to Venice. She murmured to
herself, "This man's my gondola. "[11]

What is particularly remarkable about these transfigured
experiences is that while the participants are enjoying them
they are constantly aware of the outer world. And the awareness does not impair the experiences. Just beyond the frame
of the picture described above, but not forcibly divorced from
it, is the real world with its incongruous ugliness: "she thought
well anyway I never snored or did I, it was such heaven I shan't
know unless he tells. " On the first occasion that he kisses her
there is a similar controlling awareness: "'Oh darling, ' he
said low and false, 'the months I've waited to do that!'" Again,
"She shut her eyes and settled down, not, as she told herself,
for long, to love Dickie. " The awareness is associated with,
if not partly due to, the fact that Hilly, with whom the existential experience is now enjoyed, is a very substantial member
of Roe's everyday world, as for that matter he is of hers.
She has not even the detachment of the beautiful sirens from
the upstairs flat; she is merely a member of the fire service
in an epicene uniform, tending toward fatness.
    Earlier, sex for Roe had been essentially secret. It was

associated in his mind, in a manner discussed below, with
the ice house.

> They were now on top of a hill which was not long. They came to
> where there was a hollow. Sunk in the middle of this, level with
> the turf, they found a big domed triangle of concrete. There was an
> iron door, padlocked fast. It might have been one of those houses
> in which ice used to be kept against the summer, when we had hard
> winters. In these days it was more probably a cistern to supply
> the manor house with water, but, speaking down to what he took
> to be his level of romance, Roe, in a roundabout way, said it was
> a secret, that he had never shewn anyone before, this was where
> the hob-goblins lived, no-one had ever known this place but him.
> Christopher said, "but nanny knows, Rosemary knows, oh every-
> body knows."[12]

Roe's affair with Hilly, on the other hand, is public knowledge.
The existential experience, therefore, without losing its intensity ceases to be the isolated thing that it had been. It is
ejected from the garden into the real world, where it must
earn its validity.

The relationship of outward percepts to inward postures,
discussed in connection with *Party Going*, is met again in
Caught with a new complexity. The particular and general
darkness of the early days of the war, as we have already
seen, represents the darkness traditionally associated with
the withdrawal of self-in-the-world. But the important question
concerning these and other percepts in *Caught* is not simply
whether they are literal or figurative, for they are both, but
rather to what degree are the literal things objective.[13]

There are, first, many passages that constitute imitation
in the simplest denotation of that term: small, detailed pictures
of London in the forties portray what is known and may elicit
from the reader that delight of recognition expressed in Aris-
totle's "Ah! That is he." But, if it is argued that the following
passage, for example, is a just and adequate description of the
times, suitable, say, for a government white paper or a social
history, describing the situation with only the "high simplicity
of truth," it will also be noted that there is one detail at least,
the overemphasized blueness of the girls' eyes, that modifies

the tenor of objective historic reportage and suggests another
structure.

> At that period the Fire Service came next after pilots with the
> public. Auxiliaries were often given money by old ladies, they were
> stood drinks by aged gentlemen, and, when an appeal was made
> over the wireless for blankets, there was an abundance of these
> brought in next morning. Street cleaners called Richard "mate."
> Girls looked him straight, long in the eye as never before, com-
> plicity in theirs, blue, and blue, and blue. They seemed to him
> to drag as they passed. [14]

This paragraph, though not picked at random, is enough
like many other passages to indicate that what in the novel
appears to be objective scene painting may have another or
at least an additional purpose.[15]   It is a small quotable example of the large structure of the novel in which percepts
belong to one or more of three orders, all of which are refracted through the vision of the main character.[16]   These percepts do not "reflect the subjective state of the chief character"; they do not do so, that is, literally, as, for example,
the percepts in *La tentation de saint Antoine* reflect that state
in St. Anthony. They are rather chosen by it, and they are indicative or perhaps symptomatic of it. It is curious that nearer
to Green's process than expressionism, from Webster's definition of which the above quotation is taken, is the process
Dr. Johnson finds in Milton's octosyllabic poems. His phrase
for them is curiously apposite, if we allow a maximum of
latitude in interpreting the word *gratified.* It may be seen
in them, says Johnson, "how, among the successive variety of
appearances, every disposition of mind takes hold on those
by which it may be gratified." [17]

The third order, third because it makes the most limited
appearance of the three, is that of transfigured naturalism
which makes up the descriptions of ecstasy as quoted above.
The predominant characteristics of this order are that the
percepts are vivid and that they are presented with a minimum
of relationship. This characteristic is noticeable in the passage describing Roe's garden ecstasy and more so in the ecstasy of smells in which Piper indulges.[18]

Of the other two orders, the first is constituted of percepts
only minimally distorted which may for most purposes be

considered naturalistic and which will be so designated here. This order is manifest in most of the paragraph quoted above. But in the second order the counters of the first are selected, rearranged out of their naturalistic relationships, modified, and juxtaposed according to the demands of fears and obsessions below consciousness in the mind of the protagonist. Another passage where the second order of percepts appears may well be cited: "For twenty minutes at dusk the scene was his wife's eyes, wet with tears he thought, her long lashes those black railings, everywhere wet. . . ."[19] In this sentence the integrity of the naturalistic percept has been violated by the mind that reads eyes into wet sidewalks. The principle called into play contrasts sharply with that which dominates the use of metaphor in *Party Going*. It is the principle of Coleridge's imagination, which will be discussed more fully in connection with *Back*. Meanwhile we may notice its operation once again in the domination of the protagonist's mind, with its death wish, over the two following percepts.

> Months afterwards, when the blitz began, flame came to be called "a light," they talked of "putting the light out" instead of "getting the flames down." But on those first evenings there was not one Auxiliary, fresh to the black-out, who could foresee the white flicker, then the red glow which spread and, close to, the greedy extravagance of fire which would be bombed and bombed and bombed again to increase the moth's suicide it was for firemen.[20]

> In the hard idiom of the drum these women seemed already given up to the male in uniform so soon to go away, these girls, as they felt, soon to be killed themselves, so little time left, moth deathly gay, in a daze of giving.[21]

The scenes of the novel then are for the most part of two orders of percepts both of which are refracted through Richard Roe's vision which makes its selection and arrangement in a manner gratifying to his mind. The first order of percepts may be compared with Milton's, the second order with the dream process.

Freud has described how the material of the manifest dream content is that which offers the most numerous points of contact with the greatest number of dream thoughts. Such images in the dream he calls nodal points. Each indifferent element in the dream is associated with a whole network of thoughts and occurrences of the preceding day which in turn are associated with material that for one reason or another is maintained in the mind of the dreamer at a level beneath the conscious and denied normal access thither.[22] Similarly, while all the percepts in the vision of Richard Roe are those that gratify his mind, those that belong to the second order are included because they refer back economically and immediately to his unconscious.

But it is important to point out here that, while the second order of percepts of the vision of the protagonist is selected in the same way as the elements of the dream, *Caught* is not a dream. Certain, but not all, of its percepts refer back to the mind of the protagonist at a level beneath the conscious which is normally only accessible in dreams; but the drama of the novel, unlike that of the Circe episode in *Ulysses*, for instance, is acted out at a conscious waking level. The percepts of the first order all belong to the conscious waking world; and while those of the second stand in a metaphorical or associative relationship to the abstract fears of the unconscious, they belong primarily to the first order from which they are selected. That is to say, in the paragraph already quoted the blueness must be attributed first to the naturalistic fact that the girls had blue eyes. The intensity of the blueness, signified by repetition which impairs the tenor of pure reportage, is due to the fact that blue things, blueness in general, has a metaphorical relationship to Roe's unconscious.

The percepts of the novel may be said to be within Roe's vision only in a special sense: in a general sense the novel has a shifting viewpoint and its percepts are shared among various characters. Roe, for instance, does not literally *see* what happens to Mrs. Howells in Doncaster, what happens to Pye in his dreaded visit to the asylum, or a score of other occurrences. Still less does he see Pye's memories. He has, however, a definite relationship to the percepts of the novel including the characters themselves, a relationship which is that of the novelist to his creations. It is perhaps best illustrated by supposing that Roe is trying to portray phenomena objectively in a purely objective novel, but that what gets into the novel, the particular aspects of phenomena and characters, in the particular relationships in which they appear, is what the mind selects for its gratification. The characters in *Caught* and the various phenomena are not all dream symbols; they belong to the first as well as to the second order of percepts and exist primarily in their own right. They enter Roe's vision in the manner they do, manifesting what they manifest, because they thus gratify his mind. They are his creations, then, in the sense that a figure in a historical novel is a creation of the novelist.

The concept that phenomena and characters in the novel are selected according to the mind of Roe is of particular importance in the consideration of Pye. For Pye as the creation of Roe supplies the latter with the dread that accompanies his self-creation. To some extent Freud's description of dream identities throws light upon the relationship between these two.

> There are also dreams in which my ego appears together with other persons who, when the identification is resolved, once more show themselves to be my ego. Through these identifications I shall then have to connect with my ego certain ideas to which the censorship has objected. . . . That one's ego should appear in the same dream several times or in different forms is fundamentally no more surprising than that it should appear, in conscious thinking, many times and in different places or in different relations: as, for example, in the sentence: "When *I* think what a healthy child *I* was."[23]

Pye may be regarded as the embodiment of that part of Roe's ego of which censorship, through fear, denies direct recognition. But the analogous example from conscious thinking would then be not "When I think what I was," but rather, "There but for the grace of God go I." Perhaps a better way of illustrating the relationship between the two men is by comparing it with that between Pip and Magwitch in *Great Expectations*. Here, it is pointed out, "what brings the convict Magwitch to the child Pip, in the graveyard, is more than the convict's hunger; Pip . . . carries the convict inside him, as the negative potential of his 'great expectations'—Magwitch is the concretion of his potential guilt."[24] Similarly Roe carries Pye inside him as a negative potential. Evil, as John Haye painfully learned, is internal.

Perhaps more instructive, however, of the complex relationship and no less complex interactions between these two men is the slight foreshadowing of them in the relationship between Max Adey and Embassy Richard in *Party Going.* There we have the limited identity, pointed out by Julia who, on hearing why Max dislikes Richard, "thought how odd it was that people always seemed to dislike in others just what they were always doing themselves."[25] Embassy Richard, as a conspicuous failure of the self-creating self, embodies Max's dread; and thus Max is both sympathetic and antipathetic toward him. In sympathy, he invites Richard to join the party; but in the same action, he virtually assigns him to Amabel, sexuality with whom spells annihilation of the self.

Now Pye and Roe are linked dramatically by the fact that Pye's sister had abducted Roe's son. And in a minor, non-dramatic manner they are linked by their names which, put together phonically, produce *pyro*, the Greek root for terms describing fire. But their important linkage lies in a broad similarity of career, in which Pye is a signal and monitory failure, as Roe might easily have been.

Pye is a failure in that struggle for selfhood whose terms are those that Roe contends with. Pye had had the ecstasy and had descended into the darkness. He had loved Mrs. Lane's little girl, and one afternoon in a sunny rural setting she had approached him unawares and licked jam off his mouth. Compared with Roe's it is not a very intense experience; but it is the only pleasant thing that ever happens to Pye. However, he failed to follow up or try to recreate the experience. There is an occasion when it is recalled: in the bus as Pye returns from the asylum there is a girl described in rural metaphors whom he would love to have suck jam off his mouth. But he takes no action. He chooses rather the fatal siren from the upstairs flat, Prudence, the "silky white bitch" with enameled toes, utterly unlike Mrs. Lane's little girl.

Again, Pye like Roe had entered the darkness. Now the darkness in *Caught,* as elsewhere in Green, does not entirely strip its inhabitants of their worldly selves. Private personality suffers the kind of privation familiar to anyone who has at some time given up civilian clothes for uniform; but temporal security is not entirely lost, and some activity is provided to mitigate the duress of waiting. On the other hand Pye's attitude toward the darkness is so complacent that he fails to recognize deprivation. He has fallen into the temptation of settling for darkness as a final environment and of making it do very nicely. To such a temptation Thomas Mann's Joseph succumbs, with eyes wide open as we must suppose Pye's were not; hence dark Sheol becomes garish Egypt. The complacency of these and such as these blunts the spiritual effect of darkness and neutralizes its purifying power. Thus Milton's Mammon reacts to Hell: it can be made comfortable. Pye, though less consciously, has reacted like Mammon; and in his own idiom he frequently voices the sentiment Mammon expresses in "What can Heav'n show more?"

Pye nevertheless hazards the security he has contrived to create for himself and duly loses it. Prudence, for whom he had made the sacrifice, offers only a selfish sexuality that promotes her own selfhood but denies him his. She merely uses him to relieve her tolerable misery over John, the pilot. "Of course Bert [Pye] was looking at her, and always did like that, for bed, sitting up, begging. It was different, but John would want his target so much it would really be the same. War, she thought, was sex. "[26] By such treatment, Pye loses his identity. Then he loses her, and then his job. With this final loss he enters a deeper damnation than before, a stage of profounder deprivation that John Haye, we may recall, took upon himself willingly when he left the country for London. But unlike John Haye he cannot endure it.

Here in Pye's fate is an awful example for Roe who had himself appraised Prudence. But the negative lesson to be learned concerns not only the proper kind of sexual encounter but the proper management of dread. For Pye himself endures dread. As part of the process of his own self-creation he had declined to look after his mentally deficient sister, who as a result was put into an institution. Thus the sister personifies the natural dread and guilt that accompany growth. Pye, however, never develops the sympathetic antipathy toward his dread that Kierkegaard describes. Just as John Haye had initially blamed his dread on fate, so Pye at first blames society. Later, taking responsibility for his sister's situation, he hugs his dread with fatal results.

Roe's attitude toward Pye is the proper one toward dread:

he is both sympathetic and antipathetic. But in a sense Roe may be said to be responsible for the destruction of Pye by tactics whose intention is satisfactorily cloaked before himself and others. The dust under his bed, which redounds to Roe's own discredit, is a small maneuver to discredit Pye before his superiors and hence sabotage his security. More important and resulting finally in his destruction is Roe's introduction of Pye to the sirens, purportedly a favor based on self-interest: '"I meant Pye to get off with them so I could do myself a bit of good . . . with him.'"[27] But having thus successfully destroyed him, or at least having set in motion the destructive machinery, Roe maintains, even exaggerates, his sympathy.

His compulsive solicitude before his sister-in-law at the end of the novel may be accounted for by reading it as a phenomenon of the kind of dream that Freud has described. Pye, as the creation of Roe's dream work, must be discredited and destroyed in order that he may fulfill his function with respect to Roe's ego. Freud describes a dream in which an analogous process takes place. He explains in the preface that he had been proposed for the title of *Professor Extraordinarius* which, as became apparent, while quite unaware of ambition, he desired profoundly. He assumed, however, that the investment of this honor would be denied him because he was a Jew, the identical reason that it had been denied his friend R., his academic senior. The function of the dream he describes was to overcome his waking sense of ineligibility by showing that R.'s *real* disqualification was not that he was a Jew but that he was a simpleton. But, as he analyzed the dream, the ease with which he had degraded his colleague was disquieting to Freud and led him to recall another factor in the dream, a strong feeling of affection for R., which was not one of his waking sentiments. He explains this affection as the work of the dream censor. "My dream thoughts are derogatory, and so that I may not become aware of this, the very opposite of defamation—a tender affection for him—enters into the dream."[28] In the same way, Roe, that he may not be aware of his own hostility toward Pye, is consumed with anger at his sister-in-law's.

The emergence into freedom achieved by destruction of the father figure is another important step in the growth process that Roe takes by destroying Pye. The father figure here is no stern lawgiver; and, being insidious, he is all the more dangerous an impediment. Growth for Roe, consisting partly in the recreation of the ideal love, consists also in the achievement of a self-determination which acts not according to the commands or, for that matter, the patterns of others but on its own individual account. Roe apparently does achieve at last something of such self-determination; but he pays for it, as we may by now expect, by suffering guilt feelings.

The self-determination motif is almost exclusively confined to the passages concerning the actual blitz, which serves Roe as purgatorial fire. "'That's one of the things about the blitz,' he said, getting back to himself as soon as possible, 'there's not a sub officer within sight. You just get ordered on to an address. I'm usually in charge of our pump, and you're absolutely on your own.'"[29] The recurring refrain of his description of the occasion is that there were no orders from above: "there was not one officer to report to, no-one to give orders," he says;[30] or, "no one to report to . . . I never felt so alone in all my life."[31] Alternating with this theme is that of guilt, which he feels because he is now on his own, the author of his own actions and responsible for them. The guilt is connected with his desertion of his crew when he went to find drinking water and with his subsequent, premature departure from the scene of the fire.

But the self-determination that he claims to have achieved in the blitz is of less importance as an indication of growth than the actual telling of it all. Self-determination consists here, as it does for the artist, in the creation of the work of art, in this case the narrative created by Roe and delivered to Dy.

As a work of art the narrative fails to create interest in its immediate auditor. We may note in passing that it illustrates Green's early belief that a reader's imagination might be fired by very carefully arranged passages of description.[32] For *his* audience Green supplies such passages in parentheses; and one vivid image of Roe's draws Dy's attention back to the story from which her mind had wandered.

The significance of the narrative, however, lies elsewhere. First, the narrative is not a pure report of what happened.

The parenthetic passages which edit it point out, "It had not been like that at all. "[33] Roe is aware that "'there's always something you can't describe.'"[34] The narrative, like the whole novel, is history subordinated to an order imposed upon it by Roe's immediate needs, which, to judge by the unattached emotion that haunts the story, are not entirely fulfilled. Second, the story is told compulsively: "'I do so want you to get the whole thing,'" says Roe.[35] The telling of it has cathartic and expiatory functions, which, once again, are what Green discovers for himself in his own act of writing, offering an alimentary metaphor[36] to express Kafka's *"Die Schreibung ist Geistbeschwörung."* But most important of all, the narrative works as an escape from the immediate obsession with Pye. It both describes how Roe managed to determine things on his own and, in itself as a long digression, is a tactic for evading Pye. Pye is the original topic of the conversation, of which Dy says to herself, "there he goes, he's back again. "[37] Roe forcibly shunts the conversation off in another direction. But finally it returns as it must inevitably to Pye, the topic which, in a sense, it had never left. For by negative inference it is, in fact, about Pye, whose absence, though only mentioned, is strongly felt throughout. Therefore when Dy asks at the end of the long narrative, "'I wonder what's the meaning of it all?'"[38] Roe's answer is to defend Pye bluntly and aggressively. He is ready now to rehabilitate him.

Caught is an enigmatic novel. There are strange anomalous percepts, contained rather than structurally embodied, that receive obsessive emphasis. Then there are features for which analogues may be found in the other novels and which belong to the structure that describes self-creation. But these features, the ecstasy brought to earth, the dread, the guilt, loom up unusually large and with overwhelming vividness. This strange quality which renders the otherwise familiar features so strikingly different from those in earlier novels may perhaps be related to the difference in the viewpoint from which the growth process is observed. Here in *Caught,* in a word, we see from the inside of a mind. This is not to say that in earlier novels our observation is confined to merely outward antics; for these, as already suggested, may be the figures of inward movements.

Caught, in fact, contains comparable figures. But in *Caught* they seem to be untailored and uncouth. It is as though we were experiencing an electric storm not now from an external vantage point but from within the cloud itself, where the actual phenomena themselves which cause the features that are well known at a distance are dreadful and all but unrecognizable in their proximity.

Caught also swerves from the direction established in *Living* and *Party Going*, which tended, especially the latter, to put images to metaphorical use by operation of the fancy and to prevent their despoliation. For here images are submitted to the imagination, and they lose their integrity. This change may also be related to the difference in viewpoint. But, as will be discussed further in the chapter on *Back*, imagination is in any case a necessary faculty for the recreation of the ideal past in terms of the present; "recreate" is, in fact, Coleridge's word to describe the function of the imagination.

Finally, one motif which grows in importance in later novels begins to appear in *Caught*. In the novels as a whole there are two different paradigms of behavior: characters like Richard Roe and the earlier heroes and heroines commit themselves to the darkness and the horrors of dread and guilt for the sake of creating or defending their selfhoods. But then, beginning to make an appreciable appearance in *Caught*, there are characters whose business it is, not to strike out into the unknown, but to deal as best they can with the small problems close at hand. By so doing, they maintain their comfort and they preserve their sanity.

Piper and Mrs. Howells may be briefly noted for they are so engaged. Piper, who replaces the domination of his mother-substitute wife with that of the officers in the fire service, to whom he continually crawls, makes no progress toward self-creation. He rather concentrates, by fair means or foul, upon his own comfort. Mrs. Howells prefers comfort to the assertion of herself as mother. She journeys north to confront her son-in-law whom she considers responsible for her daughter's madness. She envisages herself advancing upon the camp where the boy is stationed to come to grips with him, her righteous indignation as a mother ensuring the favor of sentries. But when she actually goes north she studiously avoids the obsess-

ing issue. She does not harangue her son-in-law as "'lazy
bastard . . . that's got no right to call yourself a man,'" as
she later claims she did.[39] On the contrary, she busies herself from the outset to find what is required for her immediate
felicity: first, tea; second, a lodging; and third, port. She
settles for fun, and the boy returns to camp hardly noticed.
For this way sanity lies.

6. LOVING

In *Caught*, as the author moves inside the mind of his protagonist, he surrenders such detachment as he had gained from
the use of irony in *Living* and *Party Going*. And so the protagonist is not of comic stature: we may sympathize with his
struggle, but we are too close to see it in perspective and too
awed either to laugh at the man or to love him very much.
Then there are emotions at large with which the author seems
to be involved and which he has failed to tether to the structure.
Whatever may cause these effects (and the author's fidelity
to a subjective history suggests itself as most likely) they are
particularly remarkable, by contrast, when we turn to *Loving*,
where a superb ease reflects a tight control of emotion and
a stern detachment from characters. Here the author is not
going to be drawn in; and comedy is ensured.

The novel, once again, is concerned with growth. Its setting
figures the early garden of childhood, adequately stocked with
mother substitutes; and it provides golden sunlight, a picnic
on the beach, the innocent joys of sexless dancing, and a background of statues of ancient Greeks for childish games. Most
important, it is withdrawn from the harsh world, partly represented by Mrs. Welch's Albert, who comes to slaughter romance and offer biological comments in counterpoint to Nanny's
pretty tale about the doves. The setting also manifests occasionally the attributes of death, darkness, and hell. There
are rooms with closed shutters and shrouded furniture, dark
corridors along which maids fear to venture, dead roses. And
much of the action takes place below ground level, where the

pros and cons of escape are debated without regard for logic.

But what the castle offers by way of death and darkness is
no means toward privation and purification. It is like the darkness in *Caught* as tamed and cultivated by Pye: merely that
comfortable environment from which the utterly unregenerate
have no ambition to flee. For that afflicting, cleansing death,
our characters must exile themselves from this unreal garden
world of Eire and embrace the terrors of blacked-out England.

The important candidate for self-creation in *Loving* is
Raunce, accompanied and spurred on by Edith. Far from this
novel are the unqualified gains made by John Haye in *Blindness* or even the qualified progress of Lily, Julia, and Richard
Roe. In the first place Raunce is an ambivalent character. His
philosophy can easily encompass the concept of a dual personality like his own: '"Miss Swift is a difficult woman whilst
she's up in her nursery. But she can be as nice as you please
outside.'"[1] Sometimes *he* is as nice as you please: young and
sprightly, quick in wit and movement. At other times he is
disgusting: old, hypochondriacal, and consumed with self-pity.
More significantly, he is both progressive and regressive; he
looks, literally and figuratively, in two directions. But even
when he is looking forward, he never sees an image of the
future without his mother in it. And it is her gathering brows,
rather than the white light of knowledge John Haye had seen,
that beacon them from the other shore when he and Edith pre-
pare to go to England.

Self-creation in this novel as in earlier ones demands the
candidate's fearful withdrawal from known conventional security into an unknown world with unfamiliar values. Such a
demand, to which Raunce eventually accedes when he quits the
castle, may be compared with the demand made of Amalia in
Kafka's *The Castle*. After the display of fire engines Amalia
is sent for by Sortini, the castle official. But the message she
receives is so obscene that she tears it up and throws it in
the face of the messenger. From then on she and the whole
family are ostracized and they fall into poverty. The implica-
tion of the long incident is that the crime for which the family
must pay was Amalia's repudiation of a relationship wherein

her selfhood could find its highest expression. She repudiated the opportunity because it appeared in terms that outraged the conventional and familiar ethics of her hitherto secure and ordinary existence. Required of her was what was required of Abraham, the suspension of the ethical, which he effected, according to Kierkegaard's exegesis, by his preparedness to sacrifice Isaac.[2]

The willing resignation of both security and temporal comfort is by now a familiar trait of Green's protagonists. Its importance as a premise for growth is re-emphasized here because at the beginning of *Loving* Raunce proceeds through a short sequence of actions which, while bearing some of the attributes of the growth process, constitute no real advance toward freedom. When old Eldon dies, Raunce takes the fearful step of assuming the other's office and his chair, an action accompanied by dread, guilt, and alienation. It is dreadful, because he fears what he himself does, as he offers his notice to Mrs. Tennant in order to get the office. But the leap from security into hazard, small though it is and fundamentally insignificant, is successful. And his immediate gain is his identity, for Mrs. Tennant begins to call him Raunce instead of the generic "Arthur." Again, in taking Eldon's chair at the table he is filled with dread at his own action. And he is at once alienated from Miss Burch; for she regrets the passing of the old man, the old conventions, the *status quo;* and she is hostile. She asks him, "Would you be in a draught?"[3] And the draught in *Loving,* though like "Siam" in *Living* it only gradually acquires full connotation, is a metaphor for guilt.

This self-advancement on the part of Raunce, though it bears certain of the now familiar attributes of self-creation, is no more than a small, self-deluding masquerade. In the first place, the self-creativity of the advance is limited by the fact that in certain parts of his new role, as is clearly indicated, Raunce is prepared to imitate his predecessor; so that in effect he is partially creating another Eldon instead of a Raunce. Furthermore the assumption of the throne of the nether empire at Kinalty, when it is achieved, is no suspension of what is familiar and secure but a consolidation of it. It gives Raunce a minor local freedom that is inimical to large freedom. He

is free to have the last word in debates, as Eldon had had.
But because he is free to have it, he is not free not to have it.
His advancement so far has led him into a cul-de-sac. His
plight may be illustrated by comparisons from both the novel
and other sources. First, the uselessness of his position is
that of Milton's Lord of Hell who asserts chieftainship to minister to pride, but who falls, in Arnold Stein's phrase, into
the "trap of leadership" and must perform actions virtually
determined by those over whom he is chief. Closer at hand
and structurally significant, Raunce's chieftainship belowstairs consists in an active sense of possession like that which
inhibits the growth of almost all the characters in the novel
belowstairs and above.

The possession of persons by others has already been noted
in earlier novels. In *Loving* possession is rife, not only of
persons but of objects: Mrs. Welch appropriates the pans,
Paddy the peacocks; Albert has his boiler; Raunce has his
Albert; Mrs. Jack is Miss Swift's "little girl"; Edith even
appropriates Mrs. Jack's adultery. In almost every case, however, as to some extent in *Living*, persons who appropriate
either objects or other persons incur reciprocal appropriation themselves with loss of freedom. The phenomenon is,
of course, not rare: as Thoreau remarked, many a man has
been drawn by his own horses. This is thoroughly exploited in
Loving, where Mrs. Tennant's possession of and by the castle
and its absurd inventory, including the servants, is the most
obvious and external instance, and Raunce's parallel appro-
priations in the underworld, especially of Edith, is the most
important.

Raunce's relationship with Edith is prominent and significant;
for the sexuality finally portended between them is a synecdoche for growth. But before their relationship may be mu-
tually conducive to self-creation each of them must undergo a
preliminary modification, in which each is the other's catalyst:
sexuality must be refined into love in him and must be awak-
ened in her. It is not enough that they merely come together
and elect each other, as the right, ready-made partners in
Party Going, and *Caught* may do. Raunce must first replace
his promiscuous sexuality with monogamous love. Early, when
Edith declines to be kissed in Mrs. Jack's primrose bathroom,

he says, "'I'll have to find the other one of you then. . . . Where is she?'" and proceeds to kiss Kate in Mrs. Tennant's blue bathroom. Such promiscuity and manifest denial of the identity of another is, of course, a denial of love. Later, when he brutally breaks in upon the girls in the ballroom, although he now has Edith specifically in mind as an object of sexuality, his action is not yet refined into love; it is still primarily selfish.

> The music came louder and louder as he progressed until at the white and gold ballroom doors it fairly thundered. He paused to look over his shoulder, with his hand on a leaping salmon trout in gilt, before pressing this lever to go in. There was no one. Nevertheless he spoke back the way he had come. "They'll break it," he said aloud as though in explanation, presumably referring to the gramophone, which was one of the first luxury clockwork models. "And in a war," he added as he turned back to these portals, "it would still fetch good money," talking to himself against the thrust of music. "The little bitches, I'll show 'em," he said and suddenly opened.[4]

This passage has been quoted by many reviewers and has been subjected to various interpretations. Without suggesting the invalidity of other readings, I wish to point out that the incident is an instance of Raunce's early, one-sided sexuality, that it is in fact symbolic rape. Earlier in the novel the sexual connotation of "salmon trout" was established. The phrase "in gilt" speaks for itself: Raunce looks over his shoulder as a guilty man, uttering his excuse to the void behind him. He breaks in bringing the squalid knowledge of who stole the water glass, which stands for fallen, worldly knowledge, and despoils the pretty scene where the innocents, childishly bent on "country pleasures," are engaged in virginal dancing among white images. His action is motivated not by love but by lust, partaking of hatred, and the desire not to share but to master and deprive (later Edith says of another thing, "'You're going to try and take that from me?'"[5]): "'The little bitches: I'll show 'em.'" In addition, Raunce's concern over the material value of the machine to the exclusion of any concern, interest, or joy in the music itself suggests that his action is scientific and lustful rather than ritualistic and loving.[6] The entry of

Edith and Kate into Paddy's private pleasure kingdom when
he is sleeping and Raunce's later coming upon Edith and the
children during the blind man's buff are not without similar
implications.

   But, partly on account of her own endeavors, Raunce's sexuality, having singled out Edith as its proper object, then becomes refined into love for her. And although his repeated
claims that he is worried about her need not be taken altogether
at face value, they need not be entirely denied. For Raunce,
the courtship is no pleasant exercise of hope and joy; and the
motive power behind it is Edith's, not his. Nevertheless, it
is Raunce himself who, though involuntarily, initiates the
relationship between them when, in the very beginning, he
looks on her unawares through the crack in the door. Edith
has been gathering peacock eggs to use to improve the luster
of her skin, the treatment being grounded in superstition rather
than science, charms for charms. The gathering of eggs is an
expression of her freedom, and she returns to the house as a
free, though stealthy, agent with a project. But Raunce is peeping; and the look upon a free agent, particularly one in a fur-
tive posture, transforms the agent into an object.[7] Raunce's
look changes Edith's status from that of a subject exercising
freedom into that of a body, a mere object, possessed now
by another. Edith's freedom, expressed in the collecting of
eggs and calculated to achieve successively beauty, attraction,
and mutual love, has now led her to being looked at as a body,
being made an object, and being possessed. Freedom has
purveyed its opposite. A similar occasion on which Raunce
unseen spies on Edith confirms their relationship as free subject and possessed body-object.

   However, Edith's sexual role with regard to Raunce is co-
operative. It is in contrast with that of Amabel in *Party Going,*
who, declining to be naked even before her lovers, avoids to
any degree being an object of anybody whomsoever. Edith's
attitude, on the other hand, is contingent upon her generosity,
which is remarkable in all her activities. For her, as for
Julia, sex is a matter of sharing. She wishes not to avoid
being an object but, at any rate in these particular circumstances and for this particular man, to be one. Then the view-
ing of her body causes the special creation of that body: the

generality, beautiful-body, to be achieved by freedom, now
without choice becomes the specific beautiful-body-for-Charley.
As Sartre says, "By virtue of consciousness the Other [that is,
the observer] is for me simultaneously the one who has stolen
my being from me and the one who causes 'there to be' a being
which is my being. "[8] In the scene in the housemaids' room
which shortly follows the peeping act, Kate, commenting on
the egg treatment, hints at the subtle metamorphosis in Edith:
"'And who's it for?'" she asks. Very soon after this, Edith
shows her own awareness of the newly created body by declar-
ing that she will not be going to see Paddy that evening.

Then she turns Raunce's discovery of her as body to her
own immediate advantage, to his embarrassment rather than
hers. When she discovers and appropriates Mrs. Jack's adultery, which, as will be discussed below, comes to figure her
own sexual maturity, she approaches Raunce with glee, willing
to share but equally willing to discomfit him. He retreats.
"'Well aren't you glad? . . . For me I mean,'" she says. And
then,

> She began once more to force her body on his notice, getting right
> up to him then away again, as though pretending to dance. Then
> she turned herself completely round in front of his very eyes. He
> seemed ill at ease. [9]

In the following passage, which is pure sport because by now
the body has fulfilled its function, the possessor is possessed
with a vengeance, and the watcher is now being watched.

> "Look," she said. She took a black silk transparent nightdress out
> of its embroidered case. "What d'you say to that Charley?"
>   He gazed, obviously struck dumb. She held it up in front of her.
> She put a hand in at the neck so that he could see the veiled skin.
> He began to breathe heavy.
>   "It's wicked, that's all," he announced at last while she watched. [10]

Raunce is now oppressed by the creation for which he was
initially responsible; the trivial act of peeping through the
door has brought upon him Edith's terrible propensity for sex.
And just as Mrs. Tennant and the others in the novel incur
reciprocal appropriation by the person or object they possess,
so Raunce as a result of his small initial possession of her

incurs a loss of his own freedom with relation to Edith. The loss, however, is merely one of local freedom; and it enables Edith to take him in hand and direct him toward a larger freedom. And before the terrors of her sexuality, representing that freedom, he very properly quails.

The vacillating progress Raunce makes as he gradually disposes himself toward self-creation is attended by guilt, objectified in great draughts of fresh air that afflict him when he is lured outside the castle. He is also the victim of dread. And dread once again is embodied in another person, this time Albert, specifically designated *his* Albert, as if to say his private problem and incubus. Like Embassy Richard in *Party Going* and Pye in *Caught,* the boy is a signal example of the failure of the self-creating self. For it is his business, as it is that of others in other novels, to re-enact ideality and integrate it with everyday reality.

Albert fails, however. His calf love for Edith furnishes him dreams, but he never succeeds in bringing them to terms with real life. He admires Edith fearfully with large eyes, and out of romantic chivalry he will tell a lie for her even though it endangers him. But he will not allow her to be anything less than a dream: even at moments of great opportunity, when Edith is lying on top of him at the picnic or when blind man's buff procures him a kiss, he is shy and retiring when he ought to be eager, active, and as heedlessly acquisitive as a pair of ragged claws. As a failure, he embodies Raunce's dread; and Raunce's attitude toward him is the familiar ambivalent one.

For himself, Raunce succeeds in a special way in recreating the pictorial ecstasy of his special rose garden. First there is the ecstasy in the library replete with rose-colored imagery, at the time of his proposition. "Lying back, he squinted into the blushing rose of that huge turf fire as it glowed, his bluer eye azure on which was a crescent rose reflection. . . . From this peat light her great eyes became invested with rose incandescence that was soft and soft and soft."[11] This ecstasy, which is necessarily fleeting, is translated into a more solid reality and one that promises more of permanence in the *picture* at the end of the novel.

What he saw then he watched so that it could be guessed that he
was in pain with his great delight. For what with the peacocks bow-
ing at her purple skirts, the white doves nodding on her shoulders
round her brilliant cheeks, and her great eyes that blinked tears
of happiness, it made a picture. [12]

But this final picture is the confirmation of another early
pictorial ecstasy, in which the picture is a wholly imaginative
one, and the ecstasy an ecstasy of pain. Raunce wants to know
from Edith whether Mr. Jack has ever kissed her. She declines to tell.

> "Oho, so that's the old game," he laughed. "Keeping me on a
> string is it, to leave me to picture this that and the other to do with
> you and him?"
> "If you can bring your imagination to such a level you're to be
> pitied," she answered tart.
> "All I did was to ask," he objected.
> "You're free to picture what you please," she replied. "I've got
> no hold on your old imagination, not yet I haven't." [13]

But in a sense she does gain a hold on his imagination. At
the end of the novel she presents him with the pictorial image
already cited, which may perhaps replace the former picture
which had been only in his imagination, and may substitute
the pain of delight for that of suspicion.

As it shows its protagonist's progress toward self-creation,
Loving apparently fits as closely as it ought a hypothetical,
developing paradigm. But the study that reveals only this much
leaves out the most interesting observation. The novel is now
to be considered in one important respect as sharply and su-
perbly anomalous with reference to its predecessors. What,
in a word, must now be questioned is whether Raunce receives
author approval, and hence reader approval, when he does the
things that he ought to do, according to values tacitly assumed
up to now, and only when he does those things.

First, approaching the matter by way of the question of
Raunce's heroism, we may consider what has so far only been
hinted at in this chapter—Edith's control of him. Early in the
novel Edith's unselfishness is established: it is she who com-

forts Kate with massage (though the debt is shortly paid) and
she who carries tea to the weeping Miss Burch. Unselfish as
she is, her guidance of Raunce is gentle. She leads him finally
out of the castle to a situation, marriage, which, according
to the terms of the novel, will be a better one for him as well
as for her. But he loses no whit of his individuality, nor is
any such loss threatened. It is he who actually makes the important decisions for both of them: what, for instance, they
shall do with the ring; that they shall elope. It is worth con-
trasting their relationship with that between Kate and Paddy,
the nature of which may be foreseen from the moment in the
stable when Edith and Kate look upon him sleeping. He becomes for them an object; and he so remains. When Kate anticipates marrying him, her intentions for him are clearly
incompatible with his individual self-creation: he is to be so
"smartened up" as to be unrecognizable. The lot of Kate, who
uses sex as an end in itself, or at least not as a means to or
part of growth, may be guessed: to be possessed by the man
she possesses, one among other peacocks.

Edith, the controlling partner and manager of Raunce's
destiny, has rightly been called the principal character in the
novel. [14] Raunce has been called the hero. [15] If Raunce *is* the
hero, he is of the kind that appears in Shakespeare's comedies:
men who are loved each by the respective heroine, managed
by her through the play, and led at the end to marriage, perhaps even to salvation. The heroism of these men consists
largely in their eligibility as prospective husbands. Similarly,
Raunce is the "hero" chiefly because he suits Edith's taste
in males.

An exploration of the limited similarity between Raunce and
Mrs. Tennant and their situations only serves to endorse the
concept that Raunce's heroism is largely Edith's endowment.
Both Raunce and Mrs. Tennant are possessors: Raunce in
his role of chieftain belowstairs, Mrs. Tennant emphatically
as the owner of the gardening glove, the sapphire cluster,
the peacocks, and the rest. The actions of both are determined
by their objects of possession. His actions assert leadership,
hers ownership. Raunce's loss of freedom consequent to possession has already been considered; Mrs. Tennant's is sufficiently manifest in a hundred details to make specific ref-

erence superfluous. Even the temple in the grounds exerts
control: the ladies feel they ought to walk that far, simply
"because it's there!" Like Mammon, Mrs. T. has gilded her
hell with marble and onyx; and she has become its janitor.
Finally, the actions of both of them, motivated by possession,
end in feathering the nest in its existing, unchanged state.

There is one important qualification to be made: Mrs. Tennant's affairs are called "actions" only to point the comparison
above. Except vicariously she is largely an inactive figure,
passively enduring chicanery, guarding the hoard. Raunce, on
the other hand, in addition to his continual management of his
Albert, is literally active on his own: the verb most often used
to describe his movements, except when he is sick, is "whip."
We cannot imagine him, except, again, when he is sick, med-
itating over grief as Mrs. Tennant is discovered to do. He has
the energy we so much admire in Joyce Cary's heroes. His
activity is not for the good in the highest sense; but we have
little hesitation in approving it rather than Mrs. Tennant's
passivity. Raunce, like Eliot's Baudelaire, is man enough to
be damned.

The important difference, however, between Raunce and
Mrs. Tennant lies in the outcome of their possessive attitudes,
in the different effects of similar causes. She, conceiving of
her total environment including the servants as objects, cannot
win sympathy over her lost ring or even a "Good afternoon."
He, conceiving of Edith as an object, starts a process of love
which is directed toward his own total salvation.

A similar distinction separates Raunce from his Albert:
Edith likes "a man that's a man and not a lad,"[16] so Albert is
ineligible for her attention. Even when he asks her advice she
declines to give it. But Albert is not merely a passive victim
of Edith's taste, which happened not to favor him, or a personality wholly determined by external causes. As already observed, he is a failure on his own account, because of his
lack of sexual initiative. But that lack of sexual initiative is,
in turn, only part of a general lack of initiative. By a wider
criterion James Hall judges Albert to be the bête noire of
Green's book because the author's sympathies are extended
to those who act and deal with the immediate and so achieve
fun, and Albert does *nothing* in situations that require *some-*

thing, and then he takes remote, "heroic" action by joining the R. A. F. [17]

Now it is when this criterion of activity is applied to Raunce that a dilemma appears and the interesting question of author approval arises. For if inaction is censured and action approved, then Raunce the "operator," in his pursuit of the immediate and in his agile, *ad hoc* reactions to circumstances, must be approved. But then if in Raunce the pursuit of the immediate and the resultant fun themselves constitute good, it is a good that ranges itself in opposition to the good of self-creation. For such actions in Raunce are directed toward his security in the castle. And in turn this security dulls, in general terms, the edge of longing for the fuller life and spells stasis, or, in local terms, it makes him comfortable and content to remain in the castle, where he is "on to a good thing" which, like the "good" that Belial found in hell, he would be happy to exploit indefinitely.

The author approval of the activities of the "operating" Raunce ought to be tested. Are these, in fact, good? Is the fun they purvey good fun or only apparently so? The acme of the fun is the laughter in the servants' hall, and it will serve for experiment. After the last of the three great shouts of laughter in the novel, Edith's "Oh it's not so bad after all"[18] voices the general sentiment. But we know that they ought not to be feeling such content, that Edith's remark is an unconscious "Evil, be thou my good." We note also that in each case the laughter is an act of exclusion. They laugh at and not with, sacrificing someone who is not present to make a Roman holiday. We know accordingly that we "ought" to consider the laughter as the paroxysmal laughter of hell which may turn at any moment into hisses, to consider it laughter that, in view of their ignorance of their own predicament, is a terror to behold. But our actual experience in reading the passages in question is not what it "ought" to be. What we experience is the intrinsic and contagious joy of the laughter, and we therefore assume the author enjoyed it too. Perhaps because we, and he, are in the same fallen state as the servants, we do not allow our awareness of the bad ethics in which the laughter is framed to spoil the fun.

Then, as we may deduce according to James Hall's criterion,

the attitude of the author has apparently changed. Earlier, human dignity, though it was rarely perfectly intact, he seemed to take for granted. In *Blindness*, John Haye spurns the security offered by his stepmother as an impediment to the realization of dreams. In *Living*, Lily quits the Craigan household where her security lies. In *Party Going*, Julia abandons well-lighted security and resolutely steps out into the darkness. In *Caught*, Richard Roe leaves his early wealthy environment for the London blackout. And there seems no question that author approval covers these and their deliberate movements; nor, conversely, does there seem to be any question that the approval is withheld from the unambitious, like the lower *bourgeoisie* in *Living* who are the objects of savage and almost gratuitous censure, and from others who conduct themselves as if comfort were the supreme value and who make ignoble terms with their environment. In this assessment, Piper and Mrs. Howells in *Caught* may be considered as occupying a neutral ground, receiving neither censure nor applause, unless Piper's final fate may be regarded as retributive. But in *Loving*, and later novels, temporal security and local fun, ends toward which characters seem to bend their energies, receive increased dispensation, while that accorded adolescent ideals wanes. The dispensation is at its height in *Concluding* where temporal security appears in the guise hitherto reserved for existential good, and sexuality figuring growth is posited not as a goal but an aberration.

It seems, in a word, that in *Loving* and thereafter, author approval is awarded not as formerly to the protagonists whose activities lead progressively through mortification to the actualization of the self but to those whose activities confirm a hitherto contemptible equilibrium.

The shift is interesting. It is as if the author had seen during the time that elapsed between, say, *Party Going* and *Loving*, during in fact six years of war, that, for human beings who cannot bear very much reality, for those who in the words of Sir Henry Harcourt-Reilly in *The Cocktail Party*, merely

> Maintain themselves by the common routine,
> Learn to avoid excessive expectation,
> Become tolerant of themselves and others,

the terrors even of stasis are sufficient unto the day. And however much or little we read into "personal disasters," the comment that Green made in 1951 is at least collateral: "It may well seem that after three wars in fifty years, counting the Boer War, and a cold war in addition, with all the reversals of fortune caused by these turmoils, not to speak of the revolutions that have taken place in the meantime, the reader has had enough of personal disasters."[19]

My comment in this last paragraph may turn from a study of effects to trespass on one of causes. But it incurs this danger in order to proscribe a greater. It is worth emphasizing that the author has only *observed* the ways of humans; he is not the moral director or assessor of the human scene. The dilemma, referred to above in order to throw into relief the duality of Raunce's situation, is a dilemma only if a moral judgment between alternatives is sought. What the novel offers and what we ought to settle for is the author's observation that men and women who are eligible for the good but dreadful undertaking of self-creation are also eligible, while ignoring or postponing the good of self-creation, for varying degrees of fun, and that fun, in the meantime, is good too. It is the author's acceptance of the possibility of a plurality of goods that marks in *Loving* the assumption of his characteristic comic stance.

A word about style may be introduced by a consideration of the figures. In its wealth of figures, *Loving* need not yield to the other novels. And while in earlier novels the fusion of the figurative expression and the dramatic is sometimes awkward, here it is not so. We have already observed in *Party Going* how the author endows a circumstance with an underlying significance; then in *Caught* Richard Roe himself apparently impresses objects and incidents with meanings gratifying to his mind. It seems in *Loving* that the characters, in a manner somewhat like Roe's, choose to find a figurative meaning, at least temporarily, in a perfectly natural circumstance. But unlike Roe, they do not thereby injure the naturalism, the impartiality, that is, of the description of objects and the disclosure of events at the dramatic level of the novel. They merely behave as real people may, in fact, be observed to behave; for much of humanity much of the time reacts to inert and emotionally neutral things with irrational joy or distress, as if they were fetishes or taboos or omens of good or evil. And it is therefore hard to say where naturalism ends or indeed that it ends at all.

What sometimes happens is what happens in *Othello* in connection with the handkerchief. Here the handkerchief becomes endowed with an importance naturally alien to it and assumes its metaphorical role signifying chastity. But only for Othello. Hence between him and Desdemona there are exchanges at cross purposes where the topic for him is the deadly serious matter of chastity, for her the trivial matter of a small article mislaid; for both it is the handkerchief. For each party the signification assumed by the other intensifies and makes stubborn the attitude inherent in his own signification.

Such exchanges abound in *Loving*. The refusal on the part of one character to accept the undisguised significance attached to an object by another is an attribute of their mutual alienation and is best illustrated in the alternate monologues that serve Miss Burch and Mrs. Welch for conversation. Certain of the private associations made and acted upon by characters, like Mrs. Jack's response to Clancarty, shared secretly by Edith, require no comment. The adultery, however, acquires metaphorical significance of particular interest. For everybody, of course, it signifies sex and therefore growth; and as such it pains static characters, Miss Burch and Miss Swift, and strikes dull fear into Raunce. For Edith, however, who more than any other is disposed toward growth, sex has no terrors. For her the discovery of the adultery signifies first a worldly maturity: now she can rank herself with Raunce who had boasted bathroom-window knowledge. Then maturity comes to signify sexual maturity in particular. And it is this fact of arrival as well as body-object that she parades before Raunce, submitting it.as her own but, strictly in character, offering to share it with him. At first she appropriates the adultery to herself; later she relinquishes her possessive interest just as she loses interest in the eggs. Her comment on the eggs accounts for both reversals: '"But the fact is now Raunce an' me's come to an understanding I got no time for charms,'"[20] the word "charms" to be read as "allurements" as Kate understands it and not as Edith intended. The body-object stage is past. Raunce, naturally enough, can understand neither her initial excitement nor her subsequent lack of interest.

The sapphire cluster has a similar extension of meaning for Edith. Like the discovery of the adultery, but perhaps more intensely, it signifies beautiful body; so she wishes to keep it for her Charley until they are married, beautiful body being the important link between them. But as beautiful body, the ring is also the tenuous link between Edith and Raunce's Albert. For Albert, both the ring and its signification are things valuable and secretly hidden; and his knowledge of them (knowledge equals knowledge), divulged to him at the picnic, becomes a burden of guilt. For the Tennant children, the ring connotes romantic attachment, as for children a ring ought; but for Mrs. Welch's Albert, the little realist, it is merely associated with procreation, and when he wishes to hide it he fittingly lays it underneath an eggshell.

The process of reading private significations into natural objects and events is one that may be generally observed among humans, but there is, in *Loving*, an important cause for it that accounts not only for the cross-purpose dialogue over the adultery and the ring but for much of the rich welter of confusion that informs the novel. In *Caught*, the mind finds gratification in laying hold on those natural objects that serve as nodal points and offer symbolic outlet for inexpressible desires and fears, so frequently linked in Green. So, in *Loving*, by a process of the same order but one that is at once more natural and more concise, characters project their desire-fears, diverting them from the objects in which they properly inhere to others where they may be made public with loss of neither face nor respectability.

Clearly Edith cannot speak literally of her body to Raunce; and still less may Albert confess in literal terms the awful knowledge he gained at the picnic. They both know, however, that in Raunce's eyes there is no terrible impropriety in theft, and thus they may speak freely in its terms. The desire for concealment, whether conscious or not, is apparent in Miss Burch's distress at Raunce's elevation at the beginning of the novel. The distress properly inheres in the fact that Eldon's dying breath had been used to mouth "Ellen" and not "Aggie."

But obviously she can make her distress public only by discovering another object for it. In the same way, Mrs. Welch
projects upon the I. R. A. her fear that the delivery of gin will
be discovered; Mrs. Tennant discusses distrust with Mrs.
Jack in terms of the servants rather than by direct reference to
the more immediate situation (although we are not really sure
how much she knows); and Kate, chagrined at losing Raunce,
fixes blame on a miscellany of causes.

These desires and fears, decently disguised, find expression
in conversation. In fact the novel resembles a stage play, in
that almost everything that happens and, equally important,
everything that does not happen is told through dialogue. As
much as it can be, the dialogue is reflective; it refers back
repeatedly to the same facts and fantasies, manifesting new
attitudes toward the same old things. Green's own comments
on dialogue are interesting. He considers it the best way of
creating "life of a kind" in a reader, because "we do not write
letters any more, we ring up on the telephone instead." Dialogue, however, is not for Green simply a means by which the
author conveys *his* facts as if they belonged to his characters.
Facts indeed are all but unknowable. When people tell us what
they have found in life, "it may be personal prejudice, but
whenever I can check up, I find they are only giving their own
version of whatever it may be." What the dialogue must do
is leave enough latitude for the reader to discover a tone that
carries the meaning, as in life it is what is left unsaid that
gives us food for thought. (Two readers may discover different tones; only "an aggregate of words . . . followed by
an action" will reveal "a glimmering of what is going on in
someone.") The author thus avoids direct communication with
his reader. He avoids it also in the stage directions that frame
the dialogue: he may describe actions, for these are unequivocal; but internal causes such as moods, fears, and the like
he may only suggest. [21]

These comments, which Green broadcast five years after
the publication of *Loving,* may nevertheless be illustrated in
this novel. Latitude, for instance, is often allowed in an absence of punctuation, giving the reader a little creative exercise. After a conversational fencing match in which Miss
Burch tries to thrust upon Miss Swift the knowledge of Mrs.

Jack's adultery, Miss Burch offers her a cup of tea. She replies, "No thank you Miss Burch all the same."[22] Such words in real life would not be uttered without a pause, so the reader has the choice of putting the pause after "No," thus emphasizing the thanks, or after the "thank you," emphasizing the denial. What in fact probably happens is that the reader keeps both possibilities in mind and holds his decision in abeyance until further speech or action confirms one or the other reading. Author withdrawal may be abundantly illustrated. The author of *Loving* knows virtually nothing except what may be heard or seen. Thoughts of characters are muttered inaudibly; motives for their actions are hesitant deductions, such as the reader himself might make, prefaced by "perhaps" or "it may be."

In his dialogue the author abides most carefully by the laws of the game he has chosen to play. And thus without stage directions or even implicit methods of telling us *exactly* how we should read this speech or that one, the fear, anger, and joy of the characters are communicated. At the same time, however, the dialogue contributes to the underlying theme of growth not only by its content, what they all say, but in the vocabulary it uses, how they all say it. In this respect the dialogue contributes appreciably to the theme of the waxing and waning of self-identity.

Each character in the novel has one or more phrases or a manner of speaking that quickly becomes distinctive. These phrases and manners are indications of the stasis of characters. There are, for instance, Miss Burch's "How's the work to get done of a morning?" Nanny's "Oh dear," Edith's "Land's sake." The fixed formulas for the static Raunce are many: "Busy Charley," "Lucky Charley," "Holy Moses," "Look sharp," and so on. His use of these indicates the old, unregenerate self in action. This self also substitutes words for epistemological adventure; the unknown can be disposed of in a phrase that will sum it all up and preclude further thought, like "the wrong side of the window" for outdoors, or, when routed and in full retreat during the incident of the nightdress, "it's wicked, that's all." The vocabulary of the old self and the obscure summary phrase are noticeably absent from his

speech or they are manifestly hollow when, as indicated by
sickness, he is undergoing the process of growth.

In Raunce's case words in themselves contribute vicariously
to security and stasis. There is a slight but interesting shift
of emphasis from words to actions at the end of the novel.
Earlier, when Kate suggests that she and Edith go back home,
Raunce cries out, "'What's all this?'" then, "'I know the name
it could be given, runnin' away, that's two words for it make
no mistake.'"[23] Later, instead of dealing with a situation by
a summary phrase, he emphasizes rather the independence of
the action from its verbal equivalent. Edith is delighted with
the word "elope." "'Why Charley,' she said, seemingly more
and more delighted, 'that's romantic.' . . . 'It's what we're
going to do, whatever the name you give it,' he replied."[24]

The characters are so little jealous of their respective selfhoods that they are willing to appropriate one another's phrases
quite freely. Such imitations occur most often as a means of
fun (fun once again inimical to the growth of selfhood). But they
also occur, not always as imitations and not always obviously,
as ready-made phrases or phrases in a ready-made style to
meet certain situations. We recall how Hamlet, resorting to
specious explanation, resorts also to the style that, in the
mouth of Polonius, has already proved itself *the* style for
speciosity. Having killed Polonius, he says,

> I do repent: but heaven hath pleased it so,
> To punish me with this and this with me.

There are comparable adoptions in *Loving.* Sometimes the
inherent fear of certain situations not only precludes immediate
individual thought and hence individual words but frightens the
speaker into the withdrawal of self that the borrowed phrase
of another implies. Edith's revelation that she has the ring
and intends to keep it frightens Raunce into answering spon-
taneously in the accent of Mrs. Welch's Albert: "'Put'm back
where you found'm.'"[25] With such an act of theft, this Albert
is naturally associated in Raunce's mind. So it is of him that
Raunce immediately thinks when he first hears that the ring
is lost: "'Maybe she put'm down and forgot to pick'm up.'"[26]

His instinct, on hearing Edith's dreadful plan, is to withdraw
from the whole situation in favor of Albert. In another situation
not quite analogous, Edith, facing the crisis with Mike Mathew-
son, jettisons her identity with '"You get off h'out,'"[27] which
was Miss Burch's admonition to the captain in an earlier crisis.

It is interesting, finally, to observe in these two aspects
of the dialogue the distance traveled since *Blindness*. There,
words reveled and multiplied, producing an unrefined emotion
as a sort of external effect; here, with the latitude in the technique by which tone is purveyed, words are sparse and controlled, not distorting, not even editing, but producing, often
by their absence, a tone revealing the heart of the matter.
Then, whereas in *Blindness* the fidelity of words to referents
was compromised, here in the dialogue words reflect not only
the spoken thoughts but the unexpressed, even unformulated,
state of mind behind them. The relation between word and
referent will be taken up once more in the next chapter where
the fidelity of words is not just an admirable aspect of style
but assumes an even more functional role.

7. BACK

The theme in *Caught*, where Richard Roe comes to recreate the garden idyl in the real world, is further explored in *Back* to form the major issue of the novel. Here the author deals once again with the proper management of the past by the self-creating protagonist. The first action of Charley Summers on returning from the war is to seek his girl in the garden of ecstasy, with its stylized roses and enameled leaves, which is also the garden of death, the churchyard. Charley's progress consists in bringing the elements of the dead garden of ecstasy into another garden which, though imperfect, having suffered the blast of bombs, is a living one. Between the roses and cypresses in both, the two gardens have much in common; but while in the dead garden the bird's nest contains addled eggs, in the living garden the nest is empty because the birds have flown. And in this garden the girl is living.

The experience in the second garden is not the end of Charley's quest because it does not lead to the endpoint of love. The evolution of Nancy counterpoints rather than harmonizes with Charley's; and Charley's quest does not end here in the living garden but is delayed, to end later with the rose garden of Nancy's nakedness. Here Nancy's quest ends too. The incompleteness of the experience in the living garden is, however, strictly a reflection of the early experience Charley enjoyed with Rose when she was alive. His memory, like Richard Roe's, a parallel in *Caught*, is an edited one. He believes that his experience with Rose was complete and that the child Ridley is his son. But Ridley is not his son; and the strong

indication is that only in nostalgic imagination was his love
for Rose consummated.

Charley's development, again like Richard Roe's, requires
not only the integration of the ideal with the real but, by other
methods, the establishment of his identity. As part of this
process the father figure, Mr. Grant, has to be destroyed.
That the destruction is effected by Charley is not unequivocally implied; all we know is that the stroke which eventually
dispatched him came upon the old man at some time after
Charley had angered him. But through the good offices of Nancy, who encourages Charley's selfhood throughout and who
leads him on as Edith led on her Charley in *Loving,* Mr. Grant
finally delivers up to Charley an opportunity for establishing
his identity.

The delivery is made in the form of clothing coupons. Personal clothing as a synecdoche for identity and uniforms for
uniformity are widely used by Green. In *Back,* Charley constantly hankers after clothing coupons; in *Party Going.* the
privation of self is indicated in the abandonment of various
items of clothing—some had not been packed, some remained
in the luggage that was left behind on the platform; Roe, in
Caught, is alienated from himself by his fireman's uniform;
sickness in Raunce, which indicates growth, grants him an
escape from uniform; Kate drags Edith's off her saying, '"It's
only your old uniform.'" And in a short story, "The Lull,"
a leitmotif that threads scenes together is the varying influence of uniform, part uniform, and mufti. [1]

In his struggle for identity Charley may also be compared
with Richard Roe because of their mutual victimization by an
incubus. The name "Middlewitch" is not complementary to
"Summers," as "Pye" is to "Roe." But it is curiously close
to Dickens' "Magwitch," in both of which the last syllable,
"witch," may be significant. This man plays a smaller part
than Pye in *Caught.* But he has as much in common with Summers as Pye with Roe, and he is dramatically linked by a similar, curious chain of coincidences. The important thing in
common to the two relationships is that both Pye and Middlewitch finally fail, and each is rehabilitated by his complementary figure.

The novel as a whole clearly has much in common with

Caught and develops certain of its themes. The similarities
ought not, however, to be allowed to obscure the fact that
Back deals essentially with a different stage in development.
I do not wish to suggest that there is any carefully tailored
paradigm underlying the novels by which various stages in
the process of self-creation may be defined as if they were
grades in a grade school. My impression is that the stages
are, indeed, very poorly defined; and I must therefore assume
that the novels do not arise from a tight system, such as the
author might have had delivered to him, complete with metaphors, through a medium. Nevertheless, it does appear that
Charley Summers is acting out a part which comes later in
the growth process than that reached by Roe; that Charley,
in a word, is back from the point where Roe is still caught.
Roe had recently relinquished his old personal life to enter
the period of privation; Charley has emerged from privation,
is re-entering the world, and is endeavoring to get back into
his individual clothing. And Charley has his souvenir, the
peg leg.

The peg leg, like John Haye's wound, is an objectification
of alienation. As well as being itself maladjusted, it clearly
figures maladjustment, the abstract, and serves to separate
Charley from other people. At the opening of the novel he is
unable to keep up with James in the churchyard, and drags
the leg awkwardly, scoring the grass; later, it serves to get
him to the head of the queue; and it is used by others to "explain" him.

The more interesting differences between *Back* and *Caught*,
however, are those arising, not from the different stages
the two novels present, but from the various techniques by
which analogous material is handled and from various emphases. In *Back,* for instance, there appears for the first
time in the novels an overt Christian allusion. Certain broad
principles which may have, to say the least, Christian connections have been alluded to in this study for the illumination
of themes in Green that they resemble structurally. It is not
supposed, however, and I hope not suggested, that the themes
in Green are Christian allegories. The novels themselves
have presented no hint of their relatedness to Christianity.
But in *Back* there is such a hint. On the occasions when Char-

ley recognizes that the idea of the dead Rose is losing its hold
on him, he is represented as "denying" her. At the beginning
of the novel Charley "knew for sure, he was to deny [her] . . .
thrice. "[2] This light suggestion envelops Charley's evolution
with a network of implications, and the question as to what
is good is again raised. Rose now temptingly, at any rate
for a passing moment, becomes the multifoliate, Christian
symbol. And the "progress" by which Charley gradually escapes from the fanatical attraction she exerts on him and replaces her with another, worldly idol is merely an expedient
of frail humanity. We find, however, that there is not, in
Back, a plurality of good like that discussed above in connection with *Loving;* in *Back*, betrayal is the good.

The word "betrayal," the Gospel word, forces the paradox.
I wish to dwell for a moment on the question of loyalty versus
betrayal because it has considerable significance in *Back*.
The apparent fallacy, of course, lies in the fact that, in contrast to the Gospel situation, the loyalty Charley breaks is to
the dead. What Charley is denying is simply an idea. His career drives him from a loyalty to the idea, the universal, to
a loyalty to the concrete; *mutatis mutandis* it is the career of
Richard Roe in *Caught*, of Lily in *Living*, and of the pigeons,
in that novel, which return to earth. It is also comparable
with the career of Jeremiah Beaumont in *World Enough and
Time*, who progresses through that novel to the point where
he can learn that although pure ideals cannot be nurtured on
the gross earth some very good things can. The career of
James Phillips, on the other hand, which is lightly touched
on in *Back*, is a movement away from the concrete toward
the abstract.

Since a Christian motif is introduced into this novel it is
perhaps worth comparing the direction of Charley's progress,
away from the ideal, with that of Pietro Spina in Ignazio Silone's *Bread and Wine;* for the comparison will suggest the
diversity of the ways by which the good may be approached.
Pietro's progress leads like Charley's away from ideals. (It
has an important and relevant philological component which
is discussed below.) The ideals are abstract plans for his
country, theoretical universals that he has incubated while
exiled from the country to which they refer. On his return,

however, he rejects these in favor of small concrete things; he learns in particular the significance of food and drink, of bread and wine. But in relinquishing the universal for the concrete he approaches it again. For bread and wine, the concretes, through their profound symbolic value, become Bread and Wine, the Concrete Universal.

In an earlier chapter of this study three methods of managing the ideal are posited: to keep it immaculate, to integrate it with the real, and to forget it altogether. Of these, the middle way is the proper one. But, among other things, *Back* is a study of various mismanagements, with which are associated various kinds of failure in perception, which in turn may amount to mania or to an austere, unimpassioned insanity.

Mrs. Grant's insanity, apparently, is at least partly a ruse, the usefulness of which to herself, while far from clear, may be in the deliverance it affords her from her husband's regimen. As madness it has only a figurative value which seems to endorse the statement above on failure in perception. The other insanities in the novel are more interesting.

James Hall observes as a generality that Green "treats the mind as a symbol-making agent ready to assimilate every object and experience to its main obsessions."[3] This process, much of the time in many of the novels, is harmless enough and even useful to the characters who indulge in it. In *Loving,* for example, it enables them to voice private concerns publicly without impropriety. In some characters, however, in other novels, the practice indicates insanity. In *Caught* the discovery, in external phenomena, of figures gratifying to the mind becomes a structural process analogous to dream work. The question of Richard Roe's sanity had better not be raised, since it must turn on any reader's personal definition; certainly, if, as I have suggested, the novel is his creation, his eye rolls in a fine frenzy and can easily suppose a bush to be a bear or assimilate what he will to his ends. The case with Pye, on the other hand, who also practices a comparable assimilation, is different: we know, if only by hindsight, that he is progressively losing sanity.

From the beginning of the novel, Pye is the victim of an *idée fixe* concerning his sister, who personifies his dread. This dread, as we have seen, is not held in careful suspen-

sion; it invades his routine life and duties. It invades his mind
even when he is making speeches, and he tries to assimilate
it. In the following he may be observed trying to contain it
in a long parenthesis. '"Take a hospital,'" Pye says, illustrating the importance of a fireman's making as little disturbance as possible: '"Go about it quietly. Don't rush in a
ward shouting where's the fire? There may be people in there
through no fault of their own. They're to be pitied.'" The dread
now begins to dominate, but it is finally contained with '"so
use your loaf.'" '"It might send them altogether crazy, a sudden shock just like that. Women that a sudden shock,' and the
whole class would laugh . . . 'Women,' Pye would go on, 'they
might be our own folks, lads, being treated lying there in bed
because of some kink, or misfortune, taken by force out of
their own homes most likely, so use your loaf.'"[4]

   In *Back,* even more than in *Caught,* the process of assimilation smacks of insanity. In these two novels insanity may be
described, first, in terms akin to those of Hall but somewhat
different, as manifesting itself very generally as the cause
and/or effect of the qualities S. T. Coleridge attributes to
the imagination, or rather as the cause-effect of these qualities run amok. The imagination, says Coleridge, "dissolves,
diffuses, dissipates, in order to recreate: or where this process is rendered impossible, yet still at all events it struggles
to idealize and to unify."[5] This faculty, useful to the poet at
work (Coleridge would say a *sine qua non*), is not by any means,
as we shall see, to be entirely discredited as a liability to
the man seeking selfhood. Its presence indicates at least his
susceptibility to sensuous impression. And, furthermore, the
re-creation he must exert upon the past is one of its powers.
Since Coleridge's terms are to be used as criteria, his term
mania may be employed for this kind of insanity.

   The most important instance of mania in *Back* is Charley's
perception of Nancy as Rose because the two have certain
identical features. Charley "struggles to idealize and to unify"
where, in and for sanity, he ought to realize and dissociate.
The working of an imagination run wild is to render a likeness
in part as a total identity. Similarly, in *Caught,* Pye unifies
where he ought to divide: he sees himself as having forced
his sister, or alternatively and with the same result, he iden-

tifies his nocturnal adventures with his sister's. As he returned from his rendezvous he saw his sister returning from hers. And here again a partial identity between two situations, an identity in time, is extended to become an identity in time *and* place that is a total identity. (What actually happened is irrelevant here.)

Charley is the victim of another kind of confusion: the word *rose,* the past tense of the verb meaning ascend, he interprets as the word for his girl, and he interprets the verb *grant* as the man. This confusion manifests a failure in Charley comparable with but distinct from the failure that causes him to think that Nancy is Rose. The misinterpretation of the word *rose* is an intellectual failure to attribute the proper referent to the sign. The other, the assumption of total identity on account of the identity of one feature but not all, which makes Nancy, Rose (or in *Caught* makes two situations identical merely because they share identity in time), is also a failure to attribute a proper referent. But it is not a sign, completely distinct from the referent, that is being misread; it is a synecdoche, insofar as a feature or features are a part of the total person whom they indicate. And, furthermore, the failure that causes the confusion between the girls is one not so much of intellect as in sensation. (The two terms *intellect* and *sensation* will serve here to distinguish the two kinds of failure. But their propriety is not beyond question; it must be especially noted that a failure *in* sensation does not imply a failure *of,* that is, an insufficiency in the faculties of perception. That kind of lack is associated rather with what I have called the intellectual failure.)

Back illustrates not only these two, the intellectual failure to find the proper referent for a sign and the failure in sensation to find it for a synecdoche, but two more. Each of the latter is a further degree of the failures in intellect and sensation described. Charley makes a wrong reference from a synecdoche, the part that should indicate the whole, and thinks that Nancy is Rose; but also, in another place, he fails to make any reference at all and regards the part as the whole. It is a small instance, but interesting. It concerns Rose's old letters to Charley, which I regard as a synecdoche rather than a sign, since they are a part of Rose and directly evoke her in a concrete manner of which the word *Rose* is not capable. Charley has destroyed these letters and is sorry that he has done so. But "he knew Nance was really Rose"—here he attributes the wrong referent to Nancy's features. Then, "after all, that had *killed* her letters."

"So, for the evening, he mourned the fact that Rose's treachery had destroyed the last there was left to him, the letters which, for all the months and years in Germany, had been what he was most afraid to find mislaid, or lost, when he got back."[6] In this passage there is a strong indication, especially in the personification, in which the letters are described as having been killed, that they, ceasing to refer back to the whole Rose of whom they are a part, have themselves become accepted as the object of love.

These two failures in sensation, then, lead respectively to a confusion as to which whole object the part refers to and to an acceptance of the part as the whole. And these failures are associated with mania. Then there are the parallel intellectual failures. The sign may refer to the wrong object, as we have seen when the words *rose* and *grant* were taken as names and not verbs; or, more seriously, the sign may refer to no object at all but be accepted itself in place of that which it ought to indicate.

Charley's muddle over Nancy and Rose and his momentary replacement of Rose by that part of her that the letters embody are caused by failures in sensation which lead to confusion of concretes; not so his failure at the office. In this instance he has impaired the efficiency of the business by substituting the abstract sign for the concrete thing. He has developed a complex card-index system to indicate, as a sign or a word, the order, arrival, and dispatch of consignments. But the sign is a failure; "'It's let you down,'" says Mr. Mead, his boss. "'Why has it? For the reason it's not accurately kept. It's untrue to the facts.'" There is a breakdown, as with the word *rose*, between the sign and its referent. But there is also implied the further kind of intellectual failure: Charley has let his card-index system, his sign, become itself the thing to which it points. Mr. Mead emphasizes the folly. "'Because I'm telling you for the last time, for your own good, you can't just put one system over another, and then be satisfied to

sit back and use the top one without any sort of a check. '"[7]
The intellectual failure, of which this trouble at the office
is a comparatively harmless result, is different from the
failure that causes the muddle over the girls. The latter is a
passionate confusion of concretes and is associated with mania;
the intellectual failure leads to an annihilation of the concrete
in favor of an abstraction (a failure, incidentally, that we
find rectified in Green's style between *Blindness* and *Living*).
And for the insanity associated with it, *mania* is not the term.
It is not the end result of Coleridge's imagination; for imagination operates under passion (in his "Dejection: An Ode" Coleridge calls it Joy) such as never was given to "the poor loveless ever-anxious crowd," and the resultant mania is caused
by a superabundance of passion. The intellectual failure, on
the other hand, is caused by a deficiency in passion and had
better be termed simply *insanity.*

The insanity along with which signs or words become things
is associated elsewhere with the mismanagement of past memories. Middlewitch provides a minor example: he lives in the
past, at least to some extent, in his continual use of French
phrases. And, we discover, his talk about sexual experience,
the talk being only the sign, is the only sexual "experience"
he knows. In even smaller instances, Mr. Mead and Mr. Grant
show that there is a link between living in the past and experiencing sex through talk.

Charley's treatment of the card index as if it were the thing
itself is a mere veniality compared with the same fault applied
to persons. Such is James Phillips' treatment of Rose. James
manifests little of the viciousness to which this treatment
may lead, as we shall see it does in *Concluding*. Meanwhile,
he provides an interesting example of an attitude which becomes more significantly villainous in the later novel. James
is one of the immensely safe: a "bloody civilian," as Charley
calls him. Such people as he studiously govern their passions
and hazard nothing; and they, when the soldiers come home
to start again, are discovered to have amassed some solid
holdings, a backlog of five years' comfortable security, and
to have acquired an easy confidence in discussing the world.
They are like those whom Conrad's typhoons pass by: lucky
but insignificant, safe but somewhat despicable.

James Phillips' perception of Rose is partial. What was Rose is now for James the abstract memory of "the best little wife a man ever had,"[8] where *little* in continual use by Middle-witch as an adjective describing women acquires a pejorative tone. Again, James says, '"Rose . . . that's my wife, who's dead and gone now, rest her soul. . . .'"[9] Features mean nothing to him: '"there's nothing to the shape of a face,'" he says; and, again, '"There's nothing in faces.'"[10] Ridley doesn't remind him of Rose; he sees no resemblance in Nancy. Rose for him is indicated not by the feature, the synecdoche, but by the abstract sign, the word. For James the flesh has become word; the concrete, abstract. James's attitude is first a denial of Rose's identity, which consists in her individuality. Denied individuality as a person, Rose may be summarily catalogued, she may be fixed as "good little wife," the "formulated phrase" of the kind used by Raunce in *Loving*, which stands as an alternative to the generous process of knowing. Second, and intimately associated with this denial, is the denial of love. James had the experience of marriage, or at least he had the comfort of it, but missed the meaning: love. Love is no doubt what he refers to as "the tripe these screwy authors serve us up with."[11] In denying the concrete, the individuality, James must perforce deny love. For love cannot inhere in nothing, the abstract, but must fix itself in lip, eye, and brow.

James's denial of love and identity may be compared with the denial of the housemaids' identities on the part of Raunce because of his early deficiency in love. James's treatment of Dot is scientific, rather than human, like Raunce's entry into the ballroom: just as Raunce approached the situation with no personal values in mind but with exclusive concern for the material value of the gramophone, so James approaches Dot exclusively as an object for sex; the girl did not know who it was until afterward.

The absence of love in one who perceives only the abstract sign and substitutes it for the totality of referent is seen also, although it is a small detail, in James's respect for Rose, paid only in abstract sign and not in the underlying referent. That is to say, he pays tribute in words, in the gesture of raising his hat to her grave, and in the voiced intention, which is clearly to remain such, of creating a pergola to her memory.

This dreadful insanity and its loveless adherence to abstracts form an important motif in at least one place in Ernest Hemingway's *A Farewell to Arms* and a pervasive motif in *Bread and Wine* A brief consideration of this motif in each of these novels serves to illuminate the significance of it as it appears in *Back* and again, larger, in *Concluding*. In a celebrated passage the hero of *A Farewell to Arms* is embarrassed at the use of the high-sounding abstracts.

I did not say anything. I was always embarrassed by the words sacred, glorious, and sacrifice and the expression in vain. We had heard them, sometimes standing in the rain almost out of earshot, so that only the shouted words came through, and had read them, on proclamations that were slapped up by billposters over other proclamations, now for a long time, and I had seen nothing sacred, and the things that were glorious had no glory and the sacrifices were like the stockyards at Chicago if nothing was done with the meat except to bury it. There were many words that you could not stand to hear and finally only the names of places had dignity. Certain numbers were the same way and certain dates and these with the names of the places were all you could say and have them mean anything. Abstract words such as glory, honor, courage, or hallow were obscene beside the concrete names of villages, the numbers of roads, the names of rivers, the numbers of regiments and the dates. [12]

There are, of course, other places in this novel where hatred of the abstract is manifest. The utterances of the battle police who are back of the lines are almost exclusively made up of abstract "obscenities." The utterances of James Phillips in *Back*, who, incidentally, is likewise back of the lines, are predominantly abstract, and the similarity here is more than mere coincidence. But the point is not that the cowardly are prone to use abstracts, "obscene" or otherwise, but that such speech is the mode of those who are not immediately in touch with the reality they are misrepresenting, whether their separation is physical or metaphysical.

With Pietro Spina, in *Bread and Wine*, a concrete physical distance figures a metaphysical one. As we have seen, Spina while abroad conceives abstract plans, and then on his return abandons them to deal with concrete realities. The manner in which these two approaches to political life are associated with two different kinds of word usage is masterly. Briefly, and to render crudely a very delicate orchestration, the heroic use of words is the most perceptive, that which is least conscious of the word itself, but, choosing with care, forces through it with least distortion a maximal revelation of the referent. The villainous use is that which surrenders its responsibility to the referent and indulges its pleasure in the sound of the word itself. The heroic attitude is seen in Spina's phrase, which has clear relevance to the problem in Green, "the thick shell of fiction and prejudice and ready-made phrases";[13] the villainous at its nadir, though parodying itself somewhat, is seen in the phrenetic cry, "Chay doo! Chay doo! Chay doo!"[14] The heroic and villainous attitudes toward words are again found in Silone's succeeding novel, *The Seed Beneath the Snow,* where, while Spina registers fear as he teaches the deaf-mute an abstract word because of the terrible distortions such words may effect, the protagonists of the "New Eloquence" are disporting themselves amid their flowery phraseology and congratulating themselves upon its superiority to facts.

There is one particular extension of this motif in *Back,* where, though small, it is more clearly stated than it is elsewhere in Green. Failure in perception is, of course, intimately related to failure in communication. The former is the cause, or following Croce the effect, of the latter. Pietro Spina's abhorrence of the ready-made phrase is partly due to its power of separating man from man. The use of an abstract idiom for communication, concomitant with the relegation of the individual to the category, is a well-known feature of contemporary utopias in fiction (and for that matter is ever present in propaganda or education departments). The generalizing process is primarily an infliction upon the individual victim. But resulting from the active failure to communicate is the passive failure to be communicated to. So James, in *Back,* who relegates personality to words is unable to hear words when these are an index of personality. Outside his house the army lorries rumble, supplying a concrete for a metaphysical cause; and Dot, who for James is only a sexual item, is unable to make herself heard.

This particular failure in communication, however, is only a special instance of a general one. In *Back,* there is a passing glance at the national scene against which the individual drama is played. And the times are out of joint. James voices the notion that everybody is off balance,[15] a notion that had in fact some popular acceptance in London at the time. The remark is made in immediate connection with Charley's mistaking Nancy for Rose. But what indicates general insanity is what indicates it in James himself—an identification of the referent with its sign.

This insanity is a small but appreciable motif in *Back*. Objects, mostly ministries, institutions, systems, and the like, are lost, particularly in the speeches of James and Mr. Grant, in the initial letters by which they are designated. And communication fails. The situation of comprehensive insanity which Charley faces is illuminated by the situation that C. S. Lewis describes in *That Hideous Strength*. Here an analogous cause brings an analogous result. The malefactors, like James, are bent on delivering up to the abstract and the general, the concrete and the individual. What they try to promote is virtually universal insanity. And what overtakes and destroys them finally is Babel, a sudden, dramatic failure in their power to communicate with each other.

Against a background of such insanity in the body politic, Charley must discover his proper means of self-creation. His business is to re-create the ecstasy and bring it to earth; he must avoid both insanity, which would preclude re-creation, and mania, which cannot come to terms with reality. His growth is impeded on the one hand by the surrounding influence of insanity and on the other by a chain of circumstances which militate in favor of his delusion. He must even strive against the author, who tricks him with an indefensible sleight of hand.

8. CONCLUDING

In *Back*, Green contrives to involve his hero, Charley Summers, more deeply in his general delusion by an exceedingly crass and melodramatic use of coincidence. Throughout the novel he offers his coincidences, one may say, quite openly. First, having described the roses in the churchyard he reveals that Charley knew a woman buried there, "and her name, of all names, was Rose. "[1] A little later Charley gets a shock when he sees who is standing near him. "For of all people, of all imaginable men . . . was James. "[2] These marked coincidences set the style. Then there are the curious links between Charley, Mr. Grant, Miss Frazier, Middlewitch, and Nancy which constitute an accumulation of coincidences somewhat less digestible than those that make the most unlikely connections in the novels of Angus Wilson. Not satisfied with these, however, Green designs by a patent sleight of hand a further and this time outrageous coincidence. At the time that Charley takes James to call on her, Nancy, for reasons carefully disclosed, is expecting the fateful knock on the door by the mobilization officer. Instead she sees James on the threshold; but she thinks he is the officer. "She took it very hard," we are told. "'So it's come,' she said, dead white, and made way. "[3] And her reaction and the conversation that follows are sufficient to drive Charley further in the delusion in which he is already far gone, that Nancy is Rose. [4]

This kind of trick is rare in Green. For though he frequently uses the surprise appearance of melodrama and the cross conversation he does not use them melodramatically, that is, to further plot. Here, however, the confounding of Charley is a somewhat important cause for later occurrences and hence a significant item in the total evolution of the novel; and it is contrived. Apart from this one instance, the manner in which Green uses the elements of melodrama is fairly consistent; and his use of them is possibly responsible for some dissatisfaction among his readers and is certainly responsible, in one novel at least, for the aftertaste of incompleteness. His way with melodrama is to arouse his readers' expectations and then to ignore them; he sets the stage, but while we await the important revelation that will conclude everything, Green concerns himself with the acting out of some other matter, making free use of the melodramatic stage properties, and leaves us at the end without finishing what he had led us to assume he had started.

In *Loving*, for example, to consider it for a moment as if we were really sensitive about having our expectations aroused all for nothing, someone *ought* to have told Mrs. Tennant about Violet's carryings on, someone *ought* to have been discharged on account of the ring, and Raunce's continual, unexpected appearances *ought* to have led to something. But if in *Loving* the writer is flirting with expectations, in *Concluding* he is virtually culpable of a breach of contract with them. This novel opens with the report of two missing girls, with a fog and a weird cry echoing through it; and it closes with one girl missing, one girl found who explains nothing, with darkness and a weird cry echoing through it. The incidents of melodrama themselves lead nowhere. They merely form a kind of framework like the naturalistic details in *Caught* upon which the significant events may be arranged.

But the great difference between *Concluding* and any of the other novels is that, while beneath the manifest drama of the others there are figurative meanings which may be called upon to provide an auxiliary rationale, in *Concluding* the drama itself is so fragmentary that figurative meanings are absolutely demanded. "The mystery," as Bruce Bain remarks, "is unanswered and the symbolism . . . is the core of the book."[5] But then the difficulty of reading figuratively is greater here than elsewhere. What James Hall observes as a generality in Green—that important symbols have a plurality of meanings and that symbols may mean different things for different characters[6]—is true as a generality. In many of the novels Green's handling of symbols forms only a manageable obstruction to reading, but in *Concluding* it is apt to be bewildering. Rather than approach the problem of the figures at once, however, we may do well to consider first the fairly clear conflict between the concrete and the abstract, the individual and the system.

The system we encounter in the state institution in *Concluding* is corrupted by the dreadful insanity already discovered in a small way in *Back* and possesses all its attributes resplendent in their vicious glory. The chief perpetrator of the insanity, and, as we shall see, its chief victim, is Edge. Her daily diet consists of such orders from above as Roe, in *Caught*, learned finally to do without; her instinct is to carry on; and her idiom is the abstract generalization, frequently written with upper-case initial letters which direct attention toward the word and away from its referent.

On the estate of the great place of which Edge is a trustee, there is a remaining outpost of individuality, Rock and his cottage. Rock has occupied it since the good old days when the whole estate, the main house of which still bears his name in Greek, was itself a privately owned rock of individuality. Edge's chronic and devouring passion is to dispossess Rock and thereby rid the estate of individuality.

But Edge's immediate victims are the girls. These are persistently denied identity and continually thought and spoken of in numbers. "Two hundred and eighty nine turned over";[7] "three hundred budding State Servants";[8] to Adams they are indistinguishable from one another; to the policeman they are "six hundred golden legs."[9] They are Ministry girls and their names all begin with M. At the dance they all wear white uniform dresses, they lift white arms to blue-veined shoulders, and there is a "slither of three hundred pairs of shoes."[10]

James Hall regards the dance and the determination of Edge that it shall be put on, come what may, as indications of her disposition toward fun and hence some small mitigation of her villainy.[11] But once again fun is inimical to growth. And it is essentially, and to a depressing extent, organized fun. "They must and shall enjoy themselves," says Edge, as if it were to be a compulsory Komsomol party in a ferromanganese plant. [12] It is above all an operation in which Edge can demonstrate and enact her supposedly benevolent autocracy by leading a uniform performance in which entity is lost in ordered harmony. It does nothing for the individuality of the girls. On the contrary, Edge, as she tells Mr. Rock, "will not be bothered tonight with individuals"; [13] and Birt and Elizabeth who manifest individual love are *de trop*. Furthermore, the dance is essentially a white and virginal entertainment; it is sexless and performed against a background of white images like the dancing of Kate and Edith in *Loving*. It is an instance of the general crippling aim of the institution to insulate its girls from knowledge, both from knowing, that is, and from being known as individuals.

Naturally the girls seek to escape from the uniformity the institution inflicts upon them and to actualize their own individual freedoms. They can achieve some sort of detachment from the institution by flaunting its rules however foolishly: the cellar is a refuge from uniformity, though in itself rather an absurd one, since its not very remarkable variety consists in the wet wine and dry coke to which the reader's attention is drawn. Then in the cellar there is the Inn, with music from the good old days of private enterprise; and there is the way out to nocturnal meetings with Adams. In rule-breaking, Mary, the missing girl, has gone one better than any of them and is therefore an object of jealousy. But what the girls seek most is to be known as concrete entities, and not merely as a great collective abstraction. For only as concrete entities are they eligible for love. And love, as shown in *Back*, can only attach itself to individual features sharply apprehended; it cannot inhere in the abstract concept of the girls maintained by Edge and to a less extent by her minions.

When the girls detach themselves from the institution they become eligible for realization as entities. The waxing of their identities is not simply due to the well-known phenomenon that girls in a crush *do* look and act alike and that they *do* tend to assume identity as they separate themselves. Those who detach themselves from the institution not only are realized as entities but are realized, more or less briefly, as objects of ecstasy.

We have seen, in *Caught* and *Back* particularly, how Green
offers a stylized pictorial representation of the object of ecstasy, bathed in incredibly intense light. Heretofore we have
been mainly interested in the subject for whom the ecstasy
materialized; but we may observe here that it is as objects
of ecstasy that Merode and Moira emerge from the uniform
crowd. Merode, who has torn her institution pajamas, perhaps
deliberately, and has carefully removed her overcoat before
calling for help, forms a brilliant picture for Sebastian, which
Elizabeth later seeks to eradicate from her lover's mind by
obvious methods.

> He looked down on a girl stretched out, whom he did not know
> to be Merode, whose red hair was streaked across a white face
> and matted by salt tears, who was in pyjamas and had one leg torn
> to the knee. A knee which, brilliantly polished over bone beneath,
> shone in this sort of pool she had made for herself in the fallen
> world of birds, burned there like a piece of tusk burnished by shift-
> ing sands, or else a wheel revolving at such speed that it had no
> edges and was white, thus communicating life to ivory, a heart
> to the still, and the sensation of a crash to this girl who lay quiet,
> reposed. [14]

To have made a place in a "fallen" world is no small achievement.

Moira's achievement of concretion, however, is more significant because we are first shown her failure to achieve
it in the institution. She makes two appearances in the novel
apart from the other girls, the first in the institution and the
second at Rock's cottage. At the former she is described from
the point of view of Marchbanks. Marchbanks is not entirely
corrupted by the state and she recognizes at least Moira's
maturity, an index of the girl's eligibility for knowledge. At
the same time her impaired vision of Moira acts entirely in
consonance with the institution ideals which deny the individual
feature. Marchbanks has removed her spectacles, so that,
although light from *outside* gives life, the description of the
girl, being the vision of an old woman with unaided eyes, is
blurred:

> . . . her bare legs [were] a gold haze to Miss Marchbanks' weak
> eyes, her figure, as the older woman thought, a rounded mass

softly merged into the exaggeration of a grown woman's, her neck
and face the colour of ripening apricots from sun with strong eyes
that were an alive blue, shapeless to Miss Marchbanks' dull poached
eggs of vision, but a child so alive, at some trick of summer light
outside, that the older woman marvelled again how it could ever be
that the State should send these girls, who were really women, to
be treated like children. . . .[15]

Later Moira appears at the cottage, the remaining strong-
hold of individuality. Rock is wearing his spectacles; he even
takes them off, cleans, and replaces them. The metaphor of
the ripening fruit is now focused and framed: her youth "made
him think of a ripe plum, on a hot day, against green leaves
on a wall." In a moment, she "nibbled at one of the azaleas
in her arms. She knew she made a picture."[16]

It is of course significant that Moira succeeds in making
herself into a picture before Rock at the cottage. For in the
conflict between individual and system he is the hero on the
side of the individual. His role is therefore to deal in concretes. Miracles for him are the warmth of the sun, which
"made it for a second so that he might have been inside a pearl
strung next the skin of his beloved";[17] the pleasurable internal
blush brought about by hot tea; and the visible and audible
delight purveyed by the descending starlings. Mr. Rock's
cottage represents the cause of individuality and concretion.
In the small incident there, Rock loves Moira for and by means
of her individual features, in a manner of loving from which
Edge and her crew are shut out.

In the consciousness of the staff, the girls appear as a group.
They appear once or twice as a flock of starlings: "The noise
of their talking was a twitter of a thousand starlings";[18] "with
a rustle of a thousand birds rising from willows about a warm
lagoon, the girls stood in silence to mark the entrance [of Edge
and Baker]."[19] The metaphor is interesting because the con-
ception of the girls as a flock begs to be considered along with
Rock's vision of the starlings returning to the treetops at
dusk, which is described in some three hundred words of superb prose at the very center of the book. Rock is enraptured;
he watches and listens. "The old man wondered, as often before, if this were not the greatest sound on earth." And then,
"'I'm glad I had that once more,' Mr. Rock said aloud."[20] But

he does not see them simply en masse. Later, it is in his consciousness that "each starling's agate eye lay folded safe beneath a wing,"[21] for his love, like God's for sparrows, concerns itself not with the mass but with each individual.

Rock, then, is the local champion of individuality and individual love. He is at the same time engaged in defending his own individuality, which depends to some extent at least on his tenure of the cottage. The chronic determination of Edge to get rid of him and secure the cottage for herself is intensified by the possibility, mentioned early in the story, that Rock may be immediately elected to the Academy of Science, variously referred to as the Institute and the scientific poor law sanatorium. Rock rigidly opposes such election, and to avoid reading the announcement of it he burns the letters which may contain it.

The cottage, which is the center and hub of the estate, is the center and hub of Rock's fears which all render themselves eventually in terms of his tenure. He says, for example, "You know the rule. . . . When one of the staff takes a wife the State always moves him to another post." But this conviction does not prevent him, on the following page, from thinking, "he was not so blind . . . spectacles or no, he could see Birt coveted the cottage, would move heaven and earth to have him sent to the Sanatorium once the ring was on her finger."[22] But while the cottage is a metaphor representing individuality for Rock and others, for him in particular it is also a metaphor representing security and stasis. And therefore, in accordance with the pattern that is by now familiar, we find him voluntarily abandoning it, albeit for a short period, to move forward through the processes of growth figured in the equally familiar descent into darkness and the sexual adventure.[23]

The dance, which is his official reason for leaving the cottage for the darkness and subsequent adventure, is first mentioned to Mr. Rock in the kitchen of the house where he is awaiting his breakfast. The girls there offer to dance with him. But the incitement to attend it really comes from Moira.

"Will you come to the dance tonight?" she asked, in a small voice.
"I might," he said. . . .

"Because, if you did, I might even give you a kiss," she continued. The chopping stopped. But he did not look up. [24]

Moira also gives him information of what is to embody the
dread that accompanies his small excursion toward self-development: Mary, she tells him, is under the water of the
lake. Shortly Rock hastens thither, taking the pig Daisy with
him. We may note not only Rock's sympathy toward his dread
but also, in the word "excuse," his guilt:

> As Mr. Rock drew near the water he was more than ever sure
> it had been a mistake to bring Daisy. . . .
> He would never get her home, he knew. She would have to be
> left to make her own way back at meal time, but there had been no
> other excuse to go down by the water, and someone had to after
> the poor girl, because those evil ninnies, whose absolute power
> so absolutely corrupted them, were too muddleheaded, or imperi-
> ous, to see what must be done in merest human charity. [25]

Guilt is manifest in the "unreasoned impulse" Rock has a moment later "that he must explain his presence, for which he
could not, he felt, account by merely saying he had taken Daisy
for a stroll."[26]

It was a mistake to bring Daisy because he is later unable
to get her back to the sty before time to go to the dance. He
goes off, therefore, leaving Daisy, his comfort and his possession, in jeopardy, just as heroes and heroines in earlier
novels hazarded their security and personal effects.

It is the "suggestion of conspiracy," again with Moira, that
induces Mr. Rock twice to go down to the cellar. That the
descent figures a sexual adventure is perfectly clear: on each
occasion a kiss qualifies him for entry; the underground passage "widened here like a green bottle from its neck"; on his
arrival on the second occasion he is handed a cup. [27] And here
he speaks of Mary, his dread. But from this place, which is
conducive to growth, Rock hastens away when he hears the
rumor that Elizabeth and Birt are engaged. He is painfully
reminded that security, the cottage, is at stake. His security
has, in fact, become encompassed and endangered by sexuality
and he is anxious to reassure himself. As he returns to the
cottage the pig appears with a dancing shoe tied round her

neck. This small metaphorical sexuality he quickly divorces from his metaphorical security and flings into the wood.

In this little excursion Rock proceeds through the rituals noted in earlier novels. Heroes and heroines hitherto, however, have been young, their ages ranging from that of John Haye in *Blindness,* who is seventeen when the novel opens, to that of Raunce, in *Loving,* who is thirty-nine. Rock is seventy-six. And if the rituals in *Concluding* are comparable in form, they are nevertheless different in value. It was pointed out in the study of *Loving* that security, comfort, and fun, with energetic activity in their procurement, were posited as an alternative good to that of growth. The good posited for Rock, though not without qualification, is not the arduous pursuit of freedom, but security and ease among possessions. Insofar as possessions possess, Rock, at seventy-six, whether or not he has grown corrupt, has grown, like Israel in the derisive phrase of Milton's Samson,

> . . . to love bondage more than liberty;—
> Bondage with ease, than strenuous liberty.

But at his age, would it have been worthwhile to reorganize his life? And would it have been safe? "Do I dare / Disturb the universe?" asks T. S. Eliot's J. Alfred Prufrock. And Mr. Rock might have asked the same question.

Thus, though in a minor way Moira makes a picture and offers an ecstasy and though he follows her through the underworld, the important picture and the important ecstasy are formed and provided by Daisy. In the following, the word *frieze,* the connotations of *cornucopia,* and the overintense coloring all suggest a picture of a pig rather than a pig.

> She lay, very white, on a froth of straw and dung which fumed to the warm of day. She was on her side and twelve most·delicate fat dugs in pink struck out from a trembling belly in a saw toothed frieze. She had violet, malevolent small eyes under pink cornucopia ears. Her corkscrew tail twitched as though its few inches could reach, in a hog's imagination, far enough to plague the brilliant, busy flies on her white, dirt dusted flanks. She was at rest. [28]

If, therefore, the picture in Green is an index of existential love, Rock's first and fundamental love is for Daisy, who is his possession and is associated, not with self-creation, but with comfort and security.

We find emerging in *Concluding* what has been hinted at earlier and what develops in importance hereafter, that security and sanity, the latter generally depending on the former, are in themselves a good and that their procurement by action is admirable. "Heroic" action in this and later novels is that which is taken with reference to immediate, local anxieties and concerns. Such action at best brings fun; and at worst it is a kind of occupational therapy which renders a character invulnerable, or more often less vulnerable, to obsessions or desire-fears that do not themselves admit of action, that overwhelm and derange the mind, and that vitiate the character's management of his proper concerns. Obsessions are joyless. They provide a precarious strength, which is illustrated in Edge; but heroes tend to avoid rather than resort to them.

These terms, by which heroism consists in countering or avoiding desires, demonstrate a shift in the author's sympathies which in earlier novels were tenderly extended to cover the young with their dreamy ideals. In these new terms adolescents fail to qualify as heroes when, like Albert in *Loving* who envisages himself remotely as an Air Force hero, they sacrifice proximate fun in favor of distant, lofty, and often impossible ideals. However, the one kind of good does not disqualify the other; self-creation through proper sexuality remains a worthy goal. Meanwhile, Mr. Rock's good solid anxieties are his animals, to the management of which he devotes his waking hours, fetching the swill, cutting wood for the fire to boil it, feeding the goose, and whatever. And they are his occupational therapy.

Most readers are prepared to accept Mr. Rock as the hero of the novel, probably because they are equally prepared to regard Edge uncompromisingly as the villain and Rock as her victim. Even though he is more sinned against than sinning, however, he too has his victims; and his villainy is worth inspection. Rock, after all, is a father figure. He is Green's "old fool," elevated to heroic rank but hardly dignified, whom we have earlier seen as Entwhistle in *Blindness,* also living in a yellow and mauve cottage; as Gates, Craigan, and Dupret senior in *Living;* as Piper, though with a difference, in *Caught;* and as Mrs. Tennant in *Loving.* All these characters seek comfort and equilibrium rather than growth. All except Piper inhibit the growth of the younger generation. Rock, according to type, inhibits growth in Elizabeth, his granddaughter.

Elizabeth is a little mad. Rock believes what Elizabeth tells Winstanley, that her derangement came from having been overworked in an institution for state servants like the one run by Edge. We may assume she has been nourished on abstractions; certainly her mental state manifests itself in a failure to communicate. "His experience with her had taught Birt," we are told, "that she took refuge in a vast quagmire of vagueness when at all pressed."[29] The hurried torrents of words that she delivers during the intermission of the dance are meaningless. For example, to a girl who had asked, in view of the plan to create a piggery on the estate, whether Daisy would like company, she replies, "'What does one, I mean it is'nt possible, is it? Animals you know. There's no way, can there be? But you see all I'm trying to say is, you may never tell, and not only with pigs when everything's told, you can't be sure of human beings, either?'"[30] The cure for her disorder depends apparently on Birt, although he thinks he caused her breakdown. She, at any rate, believes marriage will cure her. Being with him, even speaking of him, we are told, diminishes the symptoms. "It was noticeable when she spoke of this young man, and even more so when in his presence, that she was fairly collected in her talk."[31] Presumably, in the terms I have been using, if her derangement is due to having been treated as an abstract, her self-creation through love, such as that instinctively desired by the girls who dissent from the institution regulations, would be the proper cure. We may notice also incidentally, that the identity of Birt, the most versatile of all Green's mimics, needs to be established.

Rock, however, has set his mind against Elizabeth's marriage because it represents a threat to his tenure of the cottage. Elizabeth single is thus associated with his individuality and security, just as his animals are; she is, in fact, ludicrously and yet significantly identified with his sow. "I do this for Elizabeth," Rock tells himself as he goes up to the

house to get the pig swill. [32] Again, in the small interchange
between Baker and the policeman:

> It was not until they were half way, that the policeman was cer-
> tain of the pig.
> "He's got his sow along after all," he confirmed.
> "Good heavens, not his pig, surely?" Baker echoed Miss Edge,
> afraid the sergeant might be referring to Elizabeth. [33]

Finally, soon after he has taken the dancing shoe from around
Daisy's neck and flung it into the wood, he realizes that he
has deprived Liz of her dancing shoes too. Thus, conversely,
working back from Elizabeth to the pig associated with her
and thence to all the animals, we may perhaps see that Rock
is depriving them as well as his granddaughter of their sexual
opportunities. And they are all white.

The small villainy of Rock is balanced by the small heroism
in Edge. Edge is predominantly the victim and perpetrator of
institutional insanity, and she derives a precarious strength
from it. We see her often enough fortifying herself with institutional clichés, "standing guard over the Essential Good-
ness of this great Place." The public figure cannot recognize
individuality either in persons or occurrences. When, therefore, the two girls prove themselves individuals by disappear-
ing, Edge can do nothing except carry on as usual, for she is
incapable of acknowledging that events independent of her government may occur.

Back of the public Edge, however, is the private figure. And
although the emergence of this figure constitutes most often a
lapse in decorum, its existence is significant. It is the private
Edge, for instance, who can recognize Merode as a person,
can even see that in time "she is going to be extraordinarily
attractive."[34] Such recognition is merely *en passant;* the passage in which it occurs describes a strictly institutional incident—a masterly piece of inaction. But Edge is not all the
time state-minded: she can love the estate, which was called
Petra, as a thing separate from the institution; she resents the
intrusion of a piggery. Most important, she had recognized
and fostered by favoritism the individuality of Mary, the girl
who is now missing.

Mary, as individual, embodies the dread that accompanies

growth in Edge as well as in Mr. Rock. So long as Edge stays
inert, a cog in the state machine, the robot who receives directives from above and retails them to those beneath, she is
immune to dread. But she does not remain so. For it is clear
that while the cottage figures primarily the individuality that
she wishes to sweep off the estate, it is also a public figure
for a private desire. As in *Loving*, indecorous desire-fears
find respectable public embodiment, so Rock's cottage embodies with perfect propriety Edge's sexual desire for its ten-
ant. Hence Mary, dread, is almost invariably associated with
Rock, and Rock with her. The idea of self-creation through
sex brings with it continually the associated dread.

Rock is first associated with the sexual desire-fear in Edge
in the incident of the "horrid bat." Edge fears that the bat will
get into her hair and so tips the wastebasket over her head,
leaving suspended on an eyebrow a small piece of paper from
a torn-up anonymous letter on which is written "Furnicates."
Then she stoops to prevent the bat from going up her skirts.
And finally when it is gone, she remarks, '"If we could as
easily rid ourselves of Rock.'"[35] Again, the sexual connotation
of the following interchange, especially in the word *key* and in
the last sentence, is noticeable. They are discussing Rock's
election:

> "Well Edge," Miss Baker objected. "I warned you, you know,
> last night. Did'nt I? Don't lay too much store. It may not eventu-
> ate."
> "I cannot believe Providence will not provide the key after all that
> you and I have done," Edge argued. "You know what this means.
> Why, I have literally set my heart on it."[36]

Edge frequently betrays a sexual interest when she is speaking about the cottage. '"I have set my heart on it,'" for example, becomes, '"I am eating my heart out for that cottage,
Baker.'"[37] And finally, after the awful daring of the moment's
surrender when she proposes to Rock, she conceives of her
act in terms of the cottage;"—What a desperate expedient to
gain possession of a cottage, she laughed to herself."[38]

The concept of Rock as hero salted with villainy and of Edge
as the converse may suggest some kind of relationship between

them comparable with that between Pye and Roe in *Caught*. Each may conceivably be regarded as the other's alter ego. But I do not think this view is a very revealing one. On the other hand, there is a slight indication that Edge and Baker together form a composite whole. This situation may be read in a variety of trivial incidents in which the two appear to play complementary roles; it is nowhere more strongly suggested than in their joy at the first waltz when, like the two parts of man in Aristophanes' story, "they came together . . . entwined in mutual embraces, longing to grow into one."

But Aristophanes' pair were equals. Baker is probably better viewed as the public projection of the private Edge. It is she who on almost every occasion initiates human policies to deal with the absence of Mary and reacts to it in a human way: it is she who calls Merode's aunt, she who goes down to the lake, and it is she who weeps. Baker also, we are told, had a fondness for black and white things, which stand out rather obviously in the novel, like the symbols in E. M. Forster, to figure variety as opposed to uniformity. Some such relationship as that between Edge and Baker exists between Rock and Adams. Both the imputed sexuality of Adams and his paranoia are projections of these traits in Rock, while the hostility between the two men may be regarded as a *bellum intestinum* in Rock himself.

These identities are not conspicuous, but they may be considered of the same order as those that are the product of the dream work. *Concluding* has other features reminiscent of the dream. There are, for example, the many casual associations, some overt, like the one between Mr. Rock mopping his face, Miss Baker dabbing her eyes, and Mr. Dakers patting his mouth;[39] some covert, such as the one between Merode's wet mouth and Daisy's.[40] To each of these Hartleian associations, like similar ones that may be encountered elsewhere in Green, it is impossible to ascribe a specific functional significance. They do, however, provide the sensation or rather perhaps a parody of the sensation experienced by the dreamer while actually dreaming or while recollecting dreams of having been there before.

Despite the characteristic features of dreams in *Concluding*, the novel does not easily submit itself to the kind of analysis found useful in *Caught,* where the percepts refer back to the protagonist's mind. The dreamlike quality, in fact the novel as a whole, recalls the passages describing ecstasy in *Caught* where percepts are rich in *Dinglichkeit* and presented with a minimum of relationships. Most critics have declared themselves baffled by a plethora of sensations and, directing these, a limited amount of structure. Philip Toynbee may speak for them: "The world of *Concluding* is a world of pure hallucination, timeless, unhampered by the accepted sequences of cause and effect, yet strangely unified, strangely possessed of its own private logic."[41]

The following remarks are intended not as an explanation of the unusual character of the novel but as an indication of the direction such an explanation might take. The term *Dinglichkeit* used above is the term Ransom uses in distinguishing between poetry and science. Poetry, he says, tries to consist in individual things exhibited in images; poetry at its purest, Imagist poetry, is *Dinglichkeit:* "what the Imagists identified with the stuff of poetry was, simply, things." Science, on the other hand, abhors the *Dinglichkeit,* seeks the idea, and can only manage the image in terms of its own special interests.[42] Already in these two sentences the terms of the large conflict between Edge and Rock are visible. They become even clearer in the metaphor Ransom uses to define a poem.

> A poem is, so to speak, a democratic state, whereas a prose discourse—mathematic, scientific, ethical, or practical and vernacular—is a totalitarian state. The intention of a democratic state is to perform the work of state as effectively as it can perform it, subject to one reservation of conscience; that it will not despoil its members, the citizens, of the free exercise of their own private and independent characters. But the totalitarian state is interested solely in being effective, and regards the citizens as no citizens at all; that is, regards them as functional members whose existence is totally defined by their allotted contributions to its ends; it has no use for their private characters, and therefore no provision for them.[43]

Now the distinction between poetry and science, which forms a curiously relevant comment upon the major conflict in the novel, makes also an appropriate comment upon its strategy.

The novel seeks to be pure *Dinglichkeit* : the percepts exist in their own democratic right as they do in Imagist poetry. In its unwillingness to hang plot upon its sensational elements, the novel fails to be melodramatic; in its refusal to marshal its percepts and make them submit to a configuration in which they may perform the duties of structure, it fails to be dramatic. But this strategy expresses the novel's main burden. The strategy, more than any of the characters (except Mary, who does not appear), demonstrates the rights of the small concrete entity in an environment of abstracts and totalitarianism. [44]

The small consonance between the content and the technique found associated with the fancy in *Party Going* is here magnified: individuality, that aspect of growth explored most fully in *Concluding*—more fully than in any other novel—is in conflict not only with internal forces hostile to it but also with the external structure of the novel. For, just as a totalitarian government is interested in individuals only insofar as they contribute to its own purposes, so, hypothetically at least, the structure of the novel, if it is to fulfill its function as structure, must prohibit any development beyond their usefulness to the whole, of the individual details that it shapes into order. And details so curtailed may not be known as private entities. Since this function is exactly the loveless policy of scientific generalization that Edge serves and promotes, the general structure of the novel may be regarded as an aspect of her policy.

Individuality, then, opposing Edge, opposes the general structure. Mr. Rock, tempted to stray within Edge's destructive pale, has his own private structure, the diurnal round, which he insists upon for his animals and in which he himself finally rests. Other would-be individuals achieve a rebellious victory which releases them from Edge's constricting structure, but offers them no alternative.

The relation of structure to individual self-creation is seen from another angle in *Nothing* and *Doting*. Meanwhile we may notice finally in *Concluding* that if the percepts tend to defy structural organization they do not fail to produce a pronounced and fairly concordant tone. And this, in a word, is one of cruelty. With the cruelty implicit in the relationship of Rock

and Edge to their respective dependents and to each other,
the novel as a whole is informed, as an object may be charged
with static electricity. A few of the exquisitely cruel images
that lurk, like the rag doll, beneath the high midsummer pomps
will be noted to indicate the general effect. Two of these images, appearing at the end of fairly long sentences, are thus
emphasized. Two of them are unequivocally within the vision
of specific characters. The following, quoted in their order,
are only a random selection of the significantly large number
of such images in the novel. The first concerns Miss Marchbanks:

> . . . she wished to look inwards, to draw on hid reserves, and
> thus to meet the drain on her resolution which this absence of the
> two girls had opened like an ulcer high under the ribs, where it
> fluttered, a blood stained dove with tearing claws.[45]

And of Elizabeth:

> . . . [she] turned with a smile which was for him alone to let him
> take her, and helped his heart find hers by fastening her mouth on
> his as though she were an octopus that had lost its arms to the pro-
> pellers of a tug, and had only its mouth now with which, in a world
> of the hunted, to hang onto wrecked spars.[46]

Then, "At this moment Sebastian noticed the pig's outcries
for the first time. It might just have seen the knife the butcher
was about to use. "[47] Finally, "Miss Winstanley observed,
not for the first time, how a person's lipstick, when it was
smudged half way to her nose, wounded the whole face like
a bullet. "[48]

Such images and others equally cruel serve to purvey the
peculiar tone of this nightmare novel. And when we have experienced it to its full intensity, the question of what happened
to Mary shrinks to a matter of small moment.

9. NOTHING and DOTING

Nothing employs once again the themes and techniques that have been given varying emphases in earlier novels. Certain of these, in view of my earlier treatment of them, require here only a brief exposition. Their presence, however, is to be noted, even at the risk of illustrating nothing more clearly than the law of diminishing returns, in order that the fascinating shifts in their values may be demonstrated.

There are only six characters in the novel who have more than walk-on parts. And of these, it is upon Jane Weatherby and John Pomfret that interest is centered. Both belong to the old set which is determined to re-enact its prewar fun in spite of waning potency, figured in the novel by mutilated men, particularly by Arthur Morris whose toe, foot, and leg are successively amputated. John and Jane proceed through certain of the rituals already seen in earlier novels.

First of all, growth is posited for them, for Jane in particular, who alone, according to Ernest Jones, "knows what she wants and contrives to get it,"[1] in the assumption, or rather resumption, of their sexuality. The renewal of their old relationship replaces for John his "sad old affair" with the furious Liz Jennings, an affair obliquely characterized in the first scene by John's remark, "'I've *paid* haven't I? All right then, let's go back to your great bed.'"[2] For Jane, John replaces the apoplectic Richard Abbot. Liz and Richard are suitably left to each other.

Meanwhile Philip and Mary, children, respectively, of Jane and John, are contemplating marriage. This anticipated union

123

of their houses forms a figure in which the parents see their
own union. And in the incompatibility of Philip and Mary, or
in their supposed impotence for whatever reason, lies the
dread that attends the gyrations of John and Jane. At its most
intense, dread is the fear of the consanguinity of the two young
persons. It is more intense for Jane than for John: she *knows*
whether John is Philip's father. But while John is incapable of
controlled dalliance, Jane consistently succeeds in demonstrat-
ing the model treatment of dread by flirting with the ghastly
fear and yet at the same time keeping it at arm's length.

Second, *Nothing* repeats the motif in which the unreal ecstasy
becomes real. There is unreal ecstasy in a mock marriage,
with a cigar band for a ring, between John and Penelope, Jane's
six-year-old daughter, enacted in stylized, rose-colored lighting on a Sunday afternoon. Ecstasy becomes real in a wordless
community between John and Jane in the same setting and in
similar lighting.

The management of immediate anxieties with the consequent
invulnerability to obsessions, which was noted in *Concluding,*
calls for a somewhat more extensive comment. In *Nothing,*
Jane is adept at taking action in situations susceptible to it.
Her servants are a simple though minor example of manageable
concerns. On their account there is action to be taken, and
there is fun. They speak only Italian and they are of indifferent
efficiency, and Jane meets both difficulties: she learns the
language to meet the first; and she harangues them in it, to
meet the second. It is to them she turns when threatened by
unmanageable fears. There are, for instance, the occasions
when, during a conversation with John, the dread of consanguinity looms up. On the first such occasion Jane leaves her
place at the table to "twitter in bad Italian down the dumb-
waiter shaft." On the second, she handles the threat as follows:

"He [Philip] asks me the most extraordinary questions John."
"Does he now?"

"Oh I don't want to go into things" she said in haste. "Were we
like that once dear?" she asked. Then "Are we never to be served?"
she demanded with hardly a pause and in the same voice. At which
she called from the table an unintelligible phrase in which she dis-
played great confidence to be answered by an understanding, distant
shout. [3]

On both occasions it is Jane herself, characteristically flirting with dread, who has brought the fearful topic almost to the surface.

The trivial anxieties over the servants are intermittent. What possesses Jane throughout the novel is the desire to marry John and the fear of their mutual sterility, a desire-fear which, to the extent that it admits of only limited relevant action, is unmanageable. Jane can dine him, and worry over his menage, and speak with heavy innuendo of her "lonely, lonely bed"; but that is all. And for obvious reasons she can say virtually nothing in public. She deals with the desire, however, in a manner already noted in *Loving* and *Concluding*, by translating it into figurative terms that are decorous and that constitute, in addition, a manageable concern. Philip, of course, will not do for this role because he is not manageable; Jane's sexual desire-fear, therefore, is lodged with Penelope.

Penelope is a manageable concern, for her problems afford Jane opportunities for all kinds of action: she takes her to Brighton, buys her a bag to suspend from her elbow, consults a psychiatrist about her, fulfills in general and most ostentatiously the role of mother, and thus mitigates the burden of waiting. In addition to being susceptible to action, the Penelope figure allows Jane to express her dominant fear publicly in worried chatter about her daughter.

Penelope's metaphorical role is fairly clear. Note, for example, Jane's expression of an indecorous worry made decorous by means of Penelope. "'I told her the facts of life a year back, she was just five and a half then, will you believe me but she's forgotten every word, she must have done from what the little angel's said lately.'"[4] Furthermore, each of Penelope's little obsessions and cares, the grounds for Jane's anxiety over her, is a metaphorical form of one of Jane's own fears. The mutilated man at Brighton, for example, "'with a stump for an arm . . . without his coat, escaping out of chains,'"[5] is a clear and terrible image of Jane's fears about the old set with its mortality upon it but determined to live life to the lees. And no one need be as surprised as Philip is that Jane takes no notice of this obsession of Penelope's and turns away from it as deliberately as she does from Ar-

thur Morris and William Smith, another amputee. But most
of Penelope's problems and all of those that Jane herself initiates as public concerns figure more or less loosely her own
desire-fear in connection with John. There is first of all the
mock marriage, figuring the romantic desire, which bruised
little Penelope's soul and started all the other troubles; there
is the obvious and overt relation between Jane's concern over
John's diabetes and Penelope's bout of sticking pins into herself; and when at length the marriage is about to be broached
and John's financial concerns become Jane's, they are re-
flected in Penelope's overdrawn account.

The psychiatrist whom Jane consults is not permitted to
intrude so far as to see Penelope; for the little girl, although
a public metaphor, is nevertheless the metaphor of a private
concern. And except from John, Jane will hear no more advice
about her than Johnson would hear about Garrick. Finally,
when the marriage is decided upon and the desire-fear under
control, Jane, for whom Penelope's usefulness has now passed,
decides to pack her off to school.

Jane's ability to use Penelope as a metaphor and to see in
her son's love life the figure of her own depends upon the imagination which in turn depends, as in *Back*, upon passion.
There it was a superabundance of passion in Charley Summers
that led to wrong identifications. Here in Jane it is, if not a
superabundance, a generous admixture of passion that enables
her to make a controlled identity between her children's lives
and her own life. Passion is an essential element in love (a
rather obvious comment not entirely superfluous in a novel in
which a marriage without passion is anticipated), and Jane is
its grand exponent. When, therefore, she has made the limited
identity between her own life and her son's, she endeavors to
discover passion in Philip's amorous relationships which are
themselves purely hypothetical.

"No you must really have pity on the poor fainting souls Philip!
Just imagine them sitting by their telephones bored to tears with
their sad mothers who're themselves probably only dying to have
an old flame in, waiting waiting to be asked, eating their lovely
hearts out! . . .
"In a little sweat of excitement in their frocks!!"[6]

But in fact Philip is passionless, and so a literalist. When

Jane asks him, at the time they discuss the question of his
breaking the engagement, whether he has interfered with Mary,
he misunderstands: "'She was the keenest on the whole idea
as a matter of fact,'" he says. [7] Shortly afterward, he asks,
"'It's my life surely?'"; and when Jane replies, "'For you
to live if you want to live,'" he reads "live" literally: "'Of
course I wish to. I'm not ill am I?'" The passionless marriage
projected between him and Mary he accordingly envisages as
a "responsibility" and a "serious business." What he really
anticipates is no marriage at all but a sort of spinsterish association, at best a *mariage de raison*, contracted presumably
to facilitate unimpassioned Forsterian discussions about big
issues over small beer. The last view we have of him depicts
him perfectly. Mary has thrown back the ring and swept out
of the pub. Philip looks round cautiously to see if anyone has
noticed. Since no one has, he engages in a small action that
shows him completely unmoved: with the insouciance of the
torturer's horse scratching its innocent behind upon a tree,
"he finished both light ales and then left with much compo-
sure." [8]

But passion is not in itself a good unless it attaches itself
to the proper object. In this respect Richard Abbot fails, twice
when he expostulates with the waiter in the hotel at the beginning of the novel, finally when in Liz's arms he chokes and
"his staring eyes appeared to fight an enemy within." [9] Liz
too expends passion upon improper objects, most noticeably
upon Maude Winder. Jane's passion, on the other hand, is
reserved exclusively for matters of love, although it may
approach them vicariously.

It is not, however, simply propriety in object that is revealed as the condition under which passion is good; the more
important proprieties of time and place must also be observed.
And these too are violated by Liz and Abbot. In *Nothing* the
importance of the proprieties of time and place depends upon
the extreme importance of maintaining immaculate the exterior
of social transactions, maintaining, in fact, society. *Loving*
shows how decorum may be preserved by substituting for the
proper objects of concern those which may be discussed publicly with perfect propriety. The decorum in *Nothing*, preserved
by similar substitutions, is a far more significant good. And

while it is true that some aspects of Edith's love for Raunce found expression in figurative utterance, here for the first time is decorum so significant that the heroine's actual process of loving must, until the end of the book, be completely relegated to the figurative level.

Now where the question, Do I dare disturb the universe? was raised above in connection with Mr. Rock in *Concluding*, and for that matter where it was originally raised, "universe" denoted the microcosm. And the question concerned the comfortable security of the individual and the problem of whether gains consequent to its sacrifice were worth while. But if the same question were asked in connection with *Nothing*, the significant denotation of "universe" would be no microcosm but the macrocosm of society. For in *Nothing* no character is ever discovered alone, still less communing with himself, and social transactions are everything. Society is the universe at stake, and its disturbance is to be avoided at all costs. We have proceeded by now from the early situations where growth demanded the hazarding of environmental security, through situations where growth and security, though incompatible, are each a good, and through later ones where security alone is the good. In the situation that now confronts us in *Nothing* growth is a good and security is a good and they are not incompatible. The distance traveled is marked when the dereliction of environmental comfort and security on the part of Lily in *Living* or of Julia in *Party Going* is compared with the calculated exertions of Jane Weatherby to achieve the new arrangement of love relationships without disturbing her environmental security, society. Jane, in fact, while she is the most passionate of all the characters in the novel and while she leads John forward as Edith led Raunce in *Loving*, is nevertheless the champion of the cause of maintaining the perfect surface of society.

Society would rather see life steadily and, if possible, "beautifully" than see it whole; and it insistently keeps from view all but the small manageable concerns. Big things are not admissible topics: society does not speak, as Philip does, of '"making this country a place fit to live in at last,'"[10] or of "life," as Mary does. Big things must become "little," Jane's favorite word. Society will allow discussion of hats, clothes,

and jewelry; and they are important because they show. It will
not hear of mortality or consanguinity. Its anathemas are bluff
honesty, undiplomatic truth according to hard fact, and drunk-
enness. And against these it protects itself, as it may, by
wit and laughter and by a convention that permits conversation
to veer according to whim. The accepted rules of this society
are frequently violated by Dick Abbot and Liz. Dick has all
the good instincts of honor and fair play that an English public
schoolboy associates with the word "cricket" and a minimum
of sensibility and tact. His behavior at the party is characteristic: he reprehends John for his tactful withholding of Jane's
telegram, he shoves blunt facts of life into the discussion of
young girls' lodging problems, and he leaves Jane's table
when for the sake of decorum and hence of society itself, in
a special way to be discussed below, he ought to have remained. Liz is equally offensive: in particular she lets her
anger break through on occasion, she fails to conceal drunk-
enness, and at the party, Richard having left Jane's table, she
fails to join him as she should.

Passions like Liz's ought to be kept beneath the surface or
at most allowed to manifest themselves only as a faint ripple.
Jane, on the other hand, who says of Liz in private, "'she's
such a horrid beast who simply oughtn't to be alive,'"[11] greets
her socially with the conventional "darling." She strikes John,
who brings up the matter of consanguinity,[12] but she does not
act in passion; she delivers a cold, reasoned blow: "This is
Liz's doing," she says and forces him to admit it. It was not,
strictly speaking, Liz's doing. What presumably lies behind
Jane's remark is that John's breach of decorum, being due
to antisocial loss of temper, is due in turn to the influence
of Liz.

The suppression of the noxious is seconded, or possibly
initiated, by the strategy of the novel which conceals many
of its characters. There are six main and six walk-on characters; but, often representing or objectifying pain and fear,
there are no fewer than twelve named characters who do not
appear at all. In this small way the contribution of the strategy
is comparable with that seen, or rather glimpsed at, in *Concluding*. But there is besides a more significant contribution
from the external structure.

First, however, we must observe that the superficial pretti-
ness of society, which is the synecdoche for society itself and
is preserved by the methods outlined above, finds a figurative
expression in pattern. In *Nothing,* therefore, we encounter
in the content a partiality for symmetry, especially in Jane,
society's champion. Symmetry is at its splendid best in the
room decorated for the party, especially before people appear.

> Standing prepared, empty, curtained, shuttered, tall mirrors
> facing across laid tables crowned by napkins, with space rocketing
> transparence from one glass silvered surface to the other, sup-
> porting walls covered in olive-coloured silk, chandeliers repeated
> to a thousand thousand profiles to be lost in olive-grey depths as
> quiet as this room's untenanted attention. . . .[13]

The symmetry effected by the mirrors is duplicated in the
tables each set for two men and two women. Later, however,
Richard Abbot, the boor, breaks the symmetry of Jane's table
by leaving it to join another. Jane is upset; and there is nothing
except his offense in thus disturbing the symmetry, as he had
done on a previous occasion, to motivate her later complaint,
"'Oh Richard you let me down at times of crisis.'"[14] Far more
significant, however, than these elements of symmetry in the
content is the symmetry of the external structure of the novel.
In a word, not only in the texture of the novel, but in its structure, Jane Weatherby champions symmetry, and Richard Abbot, Philip, and others to a less extent despoil it.

The structural symmetry consists in matching scenes that
arrange themselves into patterns after the manner in which
rhyming lines form patterns in various stanzas or couplets.
For the purpose of illustrating this technique, I have considered as matching any two scenes in which there is an identity or a maximum of similarity between lengths, characters
involved, and topics of dialogue. In the matching of the topics
of dialogue, there is, of course, room for considerable variation within the pattern, from which is derived the same kind of
pleasure as that characteristically derived from rhyme. Two
scenes, the tenth and the eleventh, taken almost at random
from an appreciably large number of matching scenes, will
serve to illustrate. Scene 10 is a dialogue between Philip and
Mary; scene 11 is one between their parents. In the former,
broaching the topic of the conflict between generations, Philip

says, '"They all ought to be liquidated.'"[15] In the latter, John remarks, '"One's offspring are a sacred farce.'"[16] In scene 10, Philip complains that their parents' generation have done nothing but fight in two wars and that they are rotten to the core. Then Mary asks:

"Barring your relations I suppose?"
"Well Mamma's a woman. She's really not to blame. Neverthe-less I do include her. Of course she couldn't manage much about the slaughter. And she can be marvellous at times. Oh I don't know though, I think I hate them every one."[17]

The motif that hints of slaughter here is echoed in the second scene in the speech of Jane, too long to quote, describing her horror at her servant's project to procure a mouse in order to entertain the cat. Two further topics common to both scenes are the consanguinity of the juniors and Penelope's recent obsession of holding onto her elbow. Finally there is a delight-ful parallel between the end of the first of these scenes and the opening of the second. Philip, referring to a discussion between Richard Abbot and his mother about whether oxen dream, objects disgustedly to the unorthodoxy of parental conversation. Yet Jane opens the second scene by asking, "Oh my dear . . . when are we ever going to see the sun?"[18] And for a few moments she and John talk about the weather!

We may now consider the arrangement of scenes that match according to topic and/or character and/or length. Clearly the first two scenes match each other; each deals with a couple lunching in the good hotel overlooking the park, and each scene is eleven pages in length. Between them the "rhymes" abound, both in the limited descriptions that accompany the dialogues and in the topics of the dialogues themselves. And the "rhymes" are pointed in order that it may be clearly indicated from the outset that the novel proposes among its ends the pleasure derived from the play between sameness and difference. In the first scene, for instance: "He reached across and laid his hand over hers on top of the white tablecloth. Her nails were scarlet. He stroked the bare ring finger."[19] In the second scene: "Reaching across she laid a hand over his on the white tablecloth. Her nails were scarlet. She gently scratched the skin by his thumbnail."[20]

The sixth scene matches these first two. John is again with

Liz in the hotel for Sunday lunch. The match, once again, is somewhat pointed by John's anger with the waiter, restrained though it is, which echoes Abbot's earlier violence. Of the scenes between the second and the sixth, the third is incongruous and matches nothing: this is a dialogue between Philip and Mary, two whose deeds and words lack the selection and polish society requires, who contribute nothing to society and hence nothing to the pattern and symmetry dear to it. The fourth and fifth scenes match each other closely: each covers six pages and each is concerned with the parent testing the child's reaction to the suggestion of the parent's marrying again. The first six scenes, then, match as follows: AABCCA. The seventh scene, in order to preserve some kind of symmetry in the group in spite of the intrusion of the third, ought clearly to match the sixth and, in turn, the first and second. It ought, therefore, to transact a Sunday luncheon appointment between Richard Abbot and Jane. It does not do so, however. The seventh scene matches the sixth in topic, especially in the assurance given by the respective men to their women friends that the latter will one day have children; it is enacted in the hotel; and it is of approximately the same length. But in place of Richard and Jane we have Philip and Mary. Richard, therefore, having failed to take Jane to lunch, has spoiled the symmetry by his default as elsewhere he spoils internal symmetry; and Philip has usurped his mother's place in the structure.

The next four scenes are paired off into two matching "couplets." The first pair, embodying the separate visits of Mary and Philip to Brighton and to Arthur Morris, have internal matching; the second pair, the tenth and eleventh scenes studied above, conclude the first of the three parts of the novel at exactly one third of the way through.

The second part begins with the party. And here Philip's announcement of his engagement usurps his mother's place both texturally and structurally. As the party proceeds, external symmetry is destroyed along with Abbot's despoliation of the internal and Liz's flagrant breach of social decorum; "'Then you maintain I should have gone to that beastly bitch's daughter's table'"[21] exemplifies not only unsuppressed passion but a lack of sympathy for pattern.

The next seven scenes which remain in part two form no clear pattern. Their lengths vary from two pages to ten; and in the arrangement of the topics of dialogue and the characters taking part in them, no kind of formal order is discoverable. It is during these scenes that the new disposition of affections, what Richard Abbot calls the "general post," begins to be organized. And the pattern is correspondingly upset.

With the opening of the third part of the novel, however, at exactly two-thirds of the way through, patterns again appear. The first two scenes, that is, the twenty-seventh and twenty-eighth of the book, between John and Liz and John and Jane, respectively, match rather closely in topic, though not in length. Then follow five scenes, the twenty-ninth to the thirty-third, which form a pattern, AABAA. The characters and topics of these scenes are: John and Mary, consanguinity; John and Jane, consanguinity; Richard Abbot and Liz, John's diabetes (this is the incongruous middle scene enacted by an antisocial pair); John and Jane, the plan of a trip to Italy for Mary; John and Mary, Mary's prospective trip. Following this set is another of five scenes, the thirty-fourth to thirty-eighth, where the same pattern is only a little less clear. Here the incongruous middle scene is enacted by Philip and Liz. The characters in the others are respectively, Richard and Liz; John and Jane; and Richard and Liz.

The last five scenes of the novel form the pattern, AABCC. In the first are Philip and Jane, the second, Mary and John, and in both, the parents announce their marriage plans. The incongruous middle scene is between Mary and Philip in which the couple break up their marriage plans. The last two scenes are between Richard and Liz and John and Jane, respectively; and these not only match each other but match the opening scenes of the novel: Richard, for whom love is rage, gets his choking fit and goes black in the face as he had with the waiter in the hotel; and John, for whom love is peace, re-enacts with Jane the ecstasy he had had with Penelope, his topic of conversation with Liz in the first scene of the novel.

The part played by this highly artificial pattern which dominates the structure of *Nothing* and in turn the textural transactions begs to be compared with the part played by the structure in *Concluding*. In the latter we found texture successfully strug-

gling to escape from structure; Ransom's "democracy" had
become almost anarchy. For the only structure available,
not counting Mr. Rock's almost private structure, was the
totalitarian regimentation imposed by Edge. (I do not here
confuse what happens in the novel with my own reconstruction
of its strategy. The point is that what Edge wants for the end
of totalitarianism, the reader, by both his instincts for order
and his long literary experience of expectancy satisfied, is
betrayed into wanting for the end of structure. Both the reader,
because he is waiting for it, and Edge, for obvious reasons,
long for the moment of structural and totalitarian triumph
when Edge and Baker in black, holding the very center of the
room, are encircled by the waltzing girls in white pairs; similarly both reader and Edge earnestly desire the restoration
of Mary.) Structure in *Nothing,* on the other hand, is not evil
as it is in *Concluding.* It does, of course, inhibit individuality
and it does foster the stereotype. But it does so, not as an
end, but as a necessary measure toward the end of elegant
security. And here in *Nothing,* after handling the structure
somewhat roughly toward the end of part two when affections
are being redisposed, texture finds freedom, albeit a chartered
one, in accordance with structure. It does not have to run
away and live it up in the woods.

This view of society, as a kind of benevolent framework
within which growth may proceed and individuality flourish
even though its caprices are curbed, comments only upon
one aspect. It is perhaps worth observing in addition that society, that mischievous, frivolous, elegant, and banal culture,
apparently receives the approval of the author. It is, of course,
scarcely capable of anything, as John Pomfret himself admits.
It can only talk; and its talk is absurd. But even granted the
utter uselessness of these social butterflies, of their talk,
of their childish pursuit of the gay, when, as frequently happens in Green's novels, the wheel has come full circle, it is
society, the life of appearances, that wins out. Its champions,
John and Jane, find fulfillment in peaceful love with nothing
to be desired; Liz and Richard, its awkward, noncontributing
members, find a choking rage, a parody of the former; and
Philip and Mary, its open enemies, find nothing at all.

Furthermore, even if we respond with contempt to the so-

ciety portrayed, one glance at the alternative offered must
make us realize that society as it is, contemptible or not, is
not the worst possible choice. For what quite unequivocally
is worse is the alternative posited in the life and vision of
Philip Weatherby. Rather than catch the day, this unimpassioned youth believes exclusively in his work and looks forward to the unlovely prospect it offers for fifty weeks out of
the fifty-two, salted with joyless discussions in the evenings,
stretching as far as the grave. If society's pleasures are banal
and the talk mere "phatic communion," against the alternative
offered they appear desirable and even splendid. *Nothing,* in
which Ernest Jones sees the "highly stylized ritual dances of
a dying culture,"[22] is perhaps, in one respect at least, an
observation which seems to be perennial in whatever form,
that "the age of chivalry is gone. That of sophisters, econ-
mists, and calculators, has succeeded."

Now a role analogous to that played in *Nothing* by society
is played in *Doting* by marriage, which appears in the same,
not unquestionable light. Just as society in *Nothing* presents
a pretty screen which is not blemished when cruel animal
passions discover their objects behind it, so the marriage
in *Doting* is kept almost immaculate, but not quite, informing
the structure of the novel while each of its partners provides
an antithetical texture by working on, but hardly working out,
his individual salvation.

As marriage goes, marriage in the modern novel at least,
the Middletons' is a good one, if not exemplary. What had
brought them together in the first place was their dissent from
the harassment of a young man who had remarked, at a house
party, the natural perfume of a girl's hair. They discovered,
that is, a mutual agreement in their justification of ecstasy
derived from physical sensation. And since the terms on
which the marriage began are those on which it continued,
it is nurtured by physical contact and passion. But the couple also recognize the importance of money and security;
thus Diana tolerates Arthur's evenings at the desk, although
they preclude love-making, and Arthur subscribes to love-
making, although it precludes evenings at the desk. It is a
reasonable contract and, to a degree discussed below, it con-

dones extramarital expenditure of sex on his part and money on hers.

The Middletons' marriage, at first sight at any rate, appears to be kept in order more strenuously by Diana than by Arthur. Its security, like that of society in *Nothing,* is expressed in symmetry, both internal and external; and Diana works toward that symmetry. She invites Annabel, for instance, to make up the foursome at their son's first and last evenings of holidays. She resents Arthur's disturbing the furniture, two chairs and a sofa, which are arrayed, we understand, in a pattern about the fireplace. But, particularly, it is Diana who succeeds in constructing some kind of external symmetry in the sequence of scenes in the novel. These do not appear in such clear patterns as they do in *Nothing.* But there is some small triumph for symmetry in the fact that the book opens and closes with scenes matching almost exactly in length and only a little less exactly in the company, the topics of conversation, and the descriptions. That there is a second theater party at all is due to Diana. Then there is at least one set of five scenes in which the outline of a pattern is perfectly clear, a pattern that is largely the result of Diana's activities and decisions.

The set begins and ends with a scene of love-making between Diana and Arthur, the thirty-second and the thirty-sixth scenes. [23] In the three intermediate scenes Arthur and Annabel meet for dinner, and subsequently he tries and fails to seduce her; Diana makes a long-distance telephone call to Charles; Diana and Charles meet for drinks in his apartment, and subsequently he tries and fails to seduce her. Of these five scenes four are dominated by Diana who, while she obviously acts in accordance with other motives, favors the cause of symmetry. This last scene shows Diana's second rebuttal of Charles. The first rebuttal was motivated also by her sense of symmetry. She had said, "'No, Charles. Two wrongs don't make a right, do they?'"[24] But she knew that she had not really found Arthur "in bed with that horrible little Annabel Paynton," as she had said she had. [25] And therefore symmetry is better served by a qualified infidelity.

But Arthur's activities, though they appear in the above rendering to demand continual counterpoise, may themselves be regarded as restoring a symmetry that Diana has endangered.

The main threat that Arthur offers to the marriage, and in turn to structure and symmetry, is his intended treatment of Annabel, who ought to be regarded as a daughter, as a mistress. But this intended treatment is in effect only a symmetrical echo of Diana's intentions toward the boy, Peter. And she, in a sense, starts it all. Diana, characterized at the opening of the novel as "the mother, the spouse,"[26] frequently confuses the roles. As we shall see, she treats her husband as her child; and we note here that she endeavors to treat her child as her husband. An important instance of this attitude comes early in the book: she and Peter are together in the living room. She invites Peter for the sake of the light to sit in "the empty chair sacred to his father,"[27] invites him, that is, to take the role of husband. It is admittedly a small action in a small scene, but it is figuratively significant. First, in offering the "sacred" chair she prepares to violate sanctity, as Arthur later prepares to violate another sanctity. Second, offering Peter the chair, she invites him thereby to enter the light, and therefore to become an object of ecstasy.

The boy, however, declines. Later, in her effort to even the score with her husband, Diana is at a disadvantage. For this boy is only a boy (and her own boy, at that) and his instincts are still predominantly directed toward food, whereas Annabel is "out" and could and might fulfill the role of mistress. So Diana, for the sake of symmetry or "reprisals," to use her word, sends Peter off to Scotland alone and attaches to herself Charles Addinsell, who, ironically (and symmetrically), had been initially introduced into the melée by Arthur, just as Annabel had been brought in by Diana. But with this character on the scene, the doting game, which in the opening scenes of the novel had called forth only the least word of blame, ceases to be a game at all and becomes a formidable threat to the marriage.

Self-creation, as we have seen it earlier in terms of sexuality, may hardly be expected to appear without modification in this novel of marriage. Nevertheless, there are two objects in *Doting* which are set in the special lighting and described in the stylized prose hitherto reserved for objects of ecstasy. And they are significant in the highly modified growth process

upon which Arthur Middleton embarks but which he does not
finally follow through. One of these stylized passages describes
a juggling act. The floor show in the opening scene of the novel
has two features: the first, an act by a nautch girl with snakes,
is spoiled by the failure to conceal the basket in which the
snakes were conveyed to the stage. Arthur remarks, "'Per-
petrated a bit of a bloomer, surely, when they turned their
lights full on as she staggered in with the old property basket?'"[28] But the Middletons had at least watched this first
feature. When the juggler comes on, Arthur soon turns away
uninterested to devote his attention to food.

> The man started with three billiard balls. He flung one up and
> caught it. He flung it up again then sent a second ball to chase the
> first. In no time he had three, fountaining from out his hands. And
> he did not stop at that. He introduced, he insinuated one at a time,
> one more after another, and threw the exact inches higher each
> time to give six, seven balls room until, to no applause, he had a
> dozen chasing themselves up then down into his two lazy-seeming
> hands, each ball so precisely placed that it could be thought to fol-
> low grooves in violet air.[29]

Here, in the style that Green reserves for the description of
ecstatic experience, is an ideal image, removed from the
practical world of affairs.

The juggling act, in general, demonstrates ritual. And the
unconcern of Arthur, who ignores it for food, is reminiscent
of Raunce's unconcern for the music in the ballroom early
in the novel at a time when sex for him was merely appetite.
In particular the act demonstrates dexterity; what distinguished
it from the clumsy act of the nautch girl was concealment.
Whatever sleight of hand he used or for that matter whatever
exertion he paid out did not appear: in this small, brave example of *sprezzatura* he remained outwardly calm, his hands
apparently lazy. Such concealment from the senses is what
Arthur would have done well to watch and emulate. For his
marriage can tolerate a certain degree of extramarital activity
only provided that it remains out of view and virtually abstract.
"So I had nothing known," known by perception, that is, is
the condition upon which the stability and the felicity of the
marriage rest.

In the incident that occurs later, therefore, whether or not

Arthur actually had his hand on the girl's leg, his crime is rank. For it *looked* as if he had. Diana's protest derives its impetus from her outraged visual and olfactory senses: she *saw* his hand and *smelled* Annabel's perfume on him. It is appearances that count. Thus Diana, who earlier blamed Arthur for looking down the girl's corsage, concludes that it '"would be tiresome if Peter took it into his head to notice."'[30] A similar motive prevents Diana from reporting her husband to the girl's father. Again, when Arthur tells Diana that Annabel prefers older men, she demands to be told no more. '"Then, if she's said anything else of that sort, I'll thank you kindly not to tell your own wife, which I still am! One has to keep certain standards in married life, after all.'"[31] And "standards" here are appearances. Arthur recognizes and supports the same policy. Annabel is surprised to hear that he and Diana do not discuss their independent sex lives. He replies, '"If, as I say, I'm wrong to be jealous, then I'd better not know whether I've grounds for jealousy.'"[32]

The second part of the juggling act which, once again, Arthur would have done well to have studied and emulated he missed entirely. While he discussed food, there were

> . . . miracles of skill spun out a few feet beneath:—no less than the balancing of a billiard ivory ball on the juggler's chin, then a pint beer mug on top of that ball at the exact angle needed to cheat gravity, and at last the second ivory sphere which this man placed from a stick, or cue, to top all on the mug's handle:—the ball supporting a pint pot, then the pint pot a second ball until, unnoticed by our party, the man removed his chin and these separate objects fell, balls of ivory each to a hand, and the jug to a toe of his patent leather shoe where he let it hang and shine to a faint look of surprise, the artist.[33]

Here is a vision of the ideal behavior Arthur ought to have shown in reality. There is again ritual, this time complete with sex symbols of lance and grail, which Arthur, discussing food, ignores; there is the perfect action and easy elegance. Arthur's sexual endeavor, on the other hand, proves to be clumsy in both physical act and general management. He is no artist. But in this connection we must consider the second ecstasy.

The second passage written in the style reserved for ecstasy

is the description of Annabel's open mouth, and the experience
is reserved for Arthur.

> But, in spite of Mrs. Middleton's appeal, the girl, with a "here
> you are" leant over to the husband and opened wide the pearly gates.
> Her wet teeth were long and sharp, of an almost transparent white-
> ness. The tongue was pointed also and lay curled to a red tip against
> her lower jaw, to which the gums were a sterile pink. Way back
> behind, cavernous, in a deeper red, her uvula seemed to shrink
> from him. But it was the dampness, the cleanliness, the fresh-
> as-wet-paint must have made the man shut his lips tight, as, in
> his turn, he leant over hers and it was then, or so he, even, told
> his wife after, that he got, direct from her throat, a great whiff
> of flowers. [34]

Now the calm and comfortable *status quo* his marriage affords is at least in some respects a liability to Arthur. It is
precisely the environment from which Green's heroes habitually tear themselves away in order to pursue their own selfhoods. Like these heroes Arthur must escape a parentally
dominated situation; unlike them he must do so without destroying that situation. For while Diana fulfills the role of spouse
in the orthodox manner, she too frequently confuses it with
that of mother, not only in the later scenes after he has been
"naughty" but from the outset. The maternal role may be observed, for instance, in her concern with his diet at the restaurant, or in the following incident. "They were lying back
to back. Diana turned over, settled the sheets about his chin.
He brought a hand up and put these back the way they were."[35]

Furthermore, although "calm is well," it is not indeed "life's
crown." The phrases are Matthew Arnold's, and they express
the sentiment he felt after he had by his prudent marriage
with Frances Lucy insulated himself from the terror and ecstasy associated with Marguerite. As for Arnold, so for Arthur Middleton marriage had brought no final emotional settlement. While Annabel, despite the exemplary warning of her
parents' marriage, considers the institution to be the quite
perfect fulfillment of the adolescent dream, Arthur manifests,
as do other married protagonists in contemporary fiction, the
protracted hankering after an ecstasy that marriage had promised but failed to deliver. When he tells her that he spends his
lunch hour watching pretty girls, a pastime apparently as

permissible as doting over food, she says, '"But it's—it's—it's wrong!! Mind, I'm not saying people never do, nice people I mean as well, only you've no earthly need, have you, you can't have like this, as you are, if you understand. . . ."[36] Later, when Arthur tells her, '"Half the time I don't know where I am, in my emotional life I mean, whether I'm coming or going,'" she cannot believe him.

Progress in Arthur, defined in the terms of growth by now familiar, would have been marked by his re-creation in terms of reality of the ecstasy of Annabel's open mouth or of the second part of the juggling act, marked, that is, by the actual sexual experience of which the above are ideal figures. These figures he ought to have replaced with the real as John Pomfret, in *Nothing*, replaced the figurative wedding joy with the real.

There is another occurrence in *Doting*, the experience with the rabbit hutch, which is linked with the ecstasy of the open mouth by the over-all sexual implications and by many individual details. Arthur is telling Annabel of an incident that occurred when she was six. '"We discussed cleaning our teeth and got on, when no one was looking, to making terrible faces at each other,'" he says. Then, in a moment, he goes on, '"It was a big rabbit and a large hutch,'" he says.

"About three feet off the ground. You'd fixed a sloping plank so that when you turned your Doughnut out he wouldn't have to jump down. D'you recall where the hutch was, because that's everything. In the ruined chapel, on a lawn which used to be the floor, the greenest grass. I suppose you could get used to most of it but the walls, the extraordinary brick and blue ivy and stillness, absolutely not a sound, because I remember the sun was very strong that morning—well, I imagine, I shan't ever forget your rabbit twitching its nose at you while you got down on hands and knees to show me how it had to climb to get back. I thought the ladder would break under your weight, it was only elm. Then you clambered on top of the hutch, to simply become your rabbit. You crouched on the roof to show me how Doughnut, or however it was called, crouched, and the damn animal was beneath you all the time so I thought the whole thing must collapse under your weight and kill the wretched thing. All of which made me say for you to come down, but you paid no attention, and, in the end, I caught hold of your ankle to pull you off but, Ann, you screamed! Can't you remember?"[37]

This passage shows among other things that the ecstasy after

which Arthur hankers, like Diana's smaller unilateral excursion, involves the violation of sanctity as an important element: the place, the ruined chapel with the walls one could
hardly get used to, "was everything." And here there is a
little link with the description of the mouth, in which the teeth
are "pearly gates," guarding the heaven beyond.

What the ecstasies portend, however, is not the re-enactment of the beautiful thing only slightly imperfect with the
touch of the soil of the world. Because of Arthur's clumsiness,
ecstasies are reduced to the mundane when Annabel shows
her ungainly fat legs as she washes coffee off her skirt. Here
again, Arthur apparently has a hand on her leg as he had in
the incident of her childhood, and the sacred aura of the long-
remembered scene has become merely his own fatuous assumption of the kneeling posture.

The conclusion to which the above study might seem to lead
and which the last line of the novel would endorse is that no
progress is made in the novel either toward growth and self-
creation on the one hand or toward the stability of marriage
on the other. Indeed the portrayal of marriage in this the author's first full-length treatment apparently makes provision
neither for calm nor for life's crown but only for a frustrating
state of tension between the two. Such, we may be sure, must
be the conclusion concerning marriage to which Annabel Paynton, the adolescent whose dreams involve "such a vast great
deal,"[38] must come.

Once again, however, it is necessary to make a test against
alternatives offered. First there is the way Annabel arranges
her life. The nicely calculated less or more of her Hyper-
borean giving and taking in love sends her on a chronic career
of ricochet among her trivial masculine associates. She awaits,
no doubt, the palpable appearance of an ideal man; but meanwhile the practice of her ill-formulated theory of expendability,
the theory that is probably best expressed in the figurative remark, "I do eat everything,"[39] has rendered her unable to love
at all.

The important alternative to marriage, however, with its
shifting ratio of pleasure and pain so dear to Henry Green,[40]
is shown in the life of Charles Addinsell. This widower is un-

willing to remarry for fear of a second bereavement. Now
such a policy and its motivation place him among those men
and women who get short shrift in Green's later novels because, on account of remote ideals or fears, they deprive
themselves of the felicity which is at hand. In particular, he
may be associated with those on the side of villainy in *Concluding*. Charles's unwillingness to give new hostages to fortune may be read as a resignation of the proximate pleasures
that constitute the texture of life on account of his overwhelming fear of the power beyond his control which hands down the
immutable directives.

Marriage in *Doting* does not provide an absolute structure
strictly controlling licentious texture. Here marriage demands
a certain adherence, but it governs with a light rein and provides within its structure for certain private textural opera-
tions. And therefore, since a man is not wholly given over,
since there may be an operating part of the self outside the
marriage, he cannot be entirely vulnerable to fortune, to whom
he has given only hostages and not his whole self.

Our conclusion concerning marriage in *Doting*, therefore,
if only by default of the alternatives, must be that it is the
good life. (It is a much better life, incidentally, than the "good
life" of the Chamberlayne marriage in *The Cocktail Party*,
which needs the dark background of "a world of lunacy / Violence, stupidity, greed" to throw its merits into relief.) If
the evolution of the novel does not enhance the dignity of the
marriage, it does explore the permissible limits within which
textural doting may proceed. And although "the next day they
all went on very much the same, "[41] if they did not go on *quite*
the same it is because Arthur has ceased to expend sexuality
on Annabel, and Diana has begun to count the financial expense
of doting on her boy. It is significant that in the end Charles,
impressed by the Middletons' domesticity, voices a new and
friendly disposition toward the institution of marriage.

10. CONCLUSION

The studies now to be concluded rest upon the hypothesis that in each of the novels of Henry Green one or more characters adopt, relinquish, or neglect an available program of action and suffering which leads to self-creation. One important function of the hypothesis is that it links percepts and discovers structure (or perhaps a reason for the impairment of structure) in each novel and consonance in the novels as a whole. The critic must hope that he has used the hypothesis with an optimum of flexibility, for, if it is too sternly ruled, it will bow and bend and serve no function at all. But then, on the other hand, as everybody knows, a hypothesis such as this may not always be a docile beast of burden but may take the bit in its teeth and rush headlong forward.

The features of each novel, being the terms according to which self-creation is pursued, tend to be peculiar to that novel; for the process is essentially a private struggle of a private personality. Hence, each novel may be thought of as a separate species. Certain analogies between them may be discovered, as some already have been; however, the search for analogies will not reveal a genus back of the separate species but an evolutionary process in which features appear, wax in functional significance, change their functions, wane, atrophy through disuse, and disappear, or remain merely as vestigia, to make way for new features with new functions.

The great differences between the novels, however, and those that are most significant in this attempt to view the whole, are not in mutation of feature or function but in a mutation of another dimension. Not abruptly but very materially the author changes his values; or rather, the tacit approval or disapproval of the author shifts its patronage between novels from one pattern of behavior to another. And therefore what is *the* good in one novel may become *a* good in another; what is an asset may become a liability; and the liability, in that world of the later novels where "none of the characters . . . appears to have heard that man is a fallen creature, "[1] most patently becomes an asset.

I wish to study the evolution of the novels by comparing the various analogous forms of certain important features. Some comparisons of some features have already appeared *ad hoc* and piecemeal in the above studies; they will be reviewed here along with other comparisons that appear for the first time. The comparison between the analogues is partly quantitative; for, after *Blindness,* the pursuit of self-creation is nowhere engaged in with uncompromising zeal. In fact, the zeal of the protagonist is in general inversely proportional to his or her age, and age tends to increase steadily, with exceptions, as we proceed through the novels. And in certain of the later works it is the avoidance of self-creation rather than the pursuit of it that we have to observe.

First, then, I wish to study the modifications in the features of dread and guilt, which may be considered together since they are closely allied. In the earlier novels the pain caused by these features is sharper than in the later ones. Furthermore, in the earlier, dread and guilt are thrust upon the unsuspecting aspirants for self-creation as odious but inescapable burdens, whereas in the later, candidates tend, to a varying but limited degree, both to search out their own dread and guilt and to choose the figure under which these are to appear. They do so as if the attendant pains were not so much an objectionable, unavoidable feature of the growth process as a necessary, profit-bearing part. Thus the blindness, embodying dread and guilt, ineluctably thrust upon John Haye in *Blindness* and the horrors of the dreadful night in the back streets of Liverpool thrust upon Lily in *Living* may be contrasted with the analogous distress endured by Jane Weatherby and John Pomfret in *Nothing,* by Mr. Rock in *Concluding,* and in a special way by Richard Roe in *Caught.* For these later characters the pains are something less than inevitable. They choose the figures under which may appear the dread and guilt that they almost arbitrarily take upon themselves. They do so as if self-creation were a crime and as if, conscious culprits of it, they desired the beneficial infliction of a just retribution. It may also be observed of dread that, in *Loving* and *Concluding* particularly and to a less extent in other novels of the middle period, it spills over from the vessel, chosen or otherwise, that should contain it and taints other objects and situations.

Into the darkness, which represents a stage in self-creation and with which is associated loss of personal identity, John Haye and Lily are unwittingly thrust. Protagonists in *Party Going* and *Caught* seek it out and embrace it, as does Raunce in *Loving,* not without some hesitation, relinquishing the comfortable subterrane which masquerades as the dark for the real darkness of privation in blacked-out England. Darkness takes the form of the subterrane in *Concluding* where it is only lightly fearful, while in *Back, Nothing,* and *Doting* neither darkness nor any figure for it is present. It may be that in these novels characters have already reached a later stage in development. Certainly in *Back* Charley Summers seeks personal clothes, while in earlier novels divestment is a metaphor for denial of self-in-the-world.

Again, there are different degrees of horror associated with waiting. Since waiting depends upon there being something to wait for, it may hardly be considered an element in John Haye's lot; for although various compensations for loss of sight are finally bestowed upon him, he has no inkling either of them or of whatever else the future holds, and he therefore neither hopes nor waits. Waiting is horrible in the other novels only when its duration, the event awaited, or both are unknown. The duration of her waiting is unknown to Mrs. Dupret in *Living;* both duration and event are unknown in *Caught* and *Concluding.* Waiting is horrible also to the extent that its effects are unmitigated by action; for this reason it is horrible to the people in *Party Going.* Except in the novels named it is scarcely significant.

The mutual hostility between parents or parent figures and their children or wards, a most conventional feature of novels with young protagonists, undergoes interesting modification.

It is at its sharpest in *Living* where the parent actually strikes
the child, where less violently the factory and its senior of-
ficials inhibit young men, and where Dick Dupret, victim of
his father, mutters, '"Die, you old fool!"' In *Party Going* the
old aunt, with no active hostility, tends to interfere with what
the younger generation has undertaken for its self-creation.
In *Loving*, diminished parent hostility is an index of diminished
zeal for self-creation: throughout the novel, Raunce, that
epitome of fluctuation, maintains an uncomfortable filial devo-
tion. But Mrs. Tennant is also a parent figure, and toward
her he reacts according to the stereotype of the first novels.
After *Loving*, protagonists have no parents. In *Back* there
is a father figure, Mr. Grant, for whose stroke Charley Summers may be considered responsible. But thereafter the parent
hostility undergoes various strange distortions. It appears
in *Concluding* under the figure of the institution, either Edge's
or the Academy of Science against both of which Mr. Rock,
now in a kind of second childhood, asserts a fierce hostility.
In *Nothing* it is the children who enact the parental role: Philip
and Mary, inverting conventions, complain of the excesses of
the older generation; their acquiescence is sought when the
protagonists wish to marry; and, without the acrimony found
in *Living*, the war between young and old is carried on. In
Doting, the husband and wife play the role of hostile parent
to each other. And each tries to inhibit the other's efforts
at self-creation through extramarital doting.

The revolt against parent figures and against the conformity
they require results in alienation. Or, more accurately, what
happens is that when, in order to assert its freedom, the self
destroys the ties that have held it, it becomes aware of its
pre-existing and continuing loneliness. Except in two novels,
the means by which such loneliness is overcome without compromise of selfness is through sexuality. In *Blindness*, although there is a hint of sexuality between John Haye and Joan
Entwhistle, it is speech and subsequently writing that are the
means by which he breaks out of isolation. In *Concluding*, after
his sexual failure, Mr. Rock, as we shall see in another connection, is left in an isolation somewhat qualified by the community of his animals. Elsewhere alienation is defeated through
sex. In certain of the novels, as the self-creating self dis-

covers its isolation and seeks to annihilate it, it discovers
to other characters *their* isolation. [2] Then these, Kate, in
Loving, for instance, seek sexuality for themselves, although
it may be marked by expediency rather than love.

Sexuality may be conducive to growth in more than a negative
way, which merely breaks down isolation. The kind of sexuality that will promote self-creation is not just animal lust
but an expression of love, partaking of passion and ritual,
giving as well as taking. Thus in *Party Going* and *Caught,* protagonists must choose the partners with whom the right kind of
sexuality will be possible. In *Loving,* sexuality must be awak-
ened in one partner and refined into love in the other. In *Back,*
the love conducive to growth, which is developed in Charley,
contrasts sharply with the cold, calculated lust of James Phil-
ips. In *Concluding,* against a scientific background that taints
and nearly crowds out love altogether, some of the girls take
the initial step toward being loved, Birt and Elizabeth assist
the development of each other's selfhoods in mutual sexuality,
Edge and Rock make a small and worthless excursion toward
sexuality, and Adams indulges animal delight in the woods. In
Nothing, Jane and John seek and find both passion and ritual
and thence peace, Liz and Richard only passion, and Philip
and Mary neither. In the extramarital exercise of affections
in *Doting,* the ritual, with its distinctly sacred aura, is lost
in travesty. But passion subserves the marriage.

The comparison of the variously modified forms in which
security appears is of utmost significance in this account of
the evolution of the novels, for these forms are modified in
two dimensions. In earlier novels, security is a parental provision: in *Blindness, Living,* and *Party Going* it is relinquished
along with parent as an impediment to self-creation. In *Caught*
and to a less extent in *Back,* a limited security is provided
by the protagonist for himself in his work and it seems neither
to aid nor to hinder his personal development. In *Loving,* the
situation is curious: the protagonist helps to consolidate the
security furnished by the mother figure, Mrs. Tennant; and
although here once again it is a palpable impediment to his
self-creation, security is posited as an alternative good in
itself. It is a good perhaps inferior to that of growth and it
is finally relinquished in favor of the latter. But in its achieve-

ment there is a contagious, irresistible joy that may hardly be matched in fiction. In *Concluding* Mr. Rock's security is relinquished as he briefly proceeds through the rituals of growth. But in the old man security is the asset to and growth a divergence from the good. Security in *Nothing* is provided by society, and the protagonists nourish it as Mr. Rock nourishes his. But here, on the other hand, security is not essentially incompatible with self-creation, which John and Jane pursue without jeopardizing it. In *Doting,* marriage constitutes the security, which the Middletons endanger without seeming to achieve any appreciable growth.

Next, I wish to study throughout the novels the modifications in a process common to almost all of them by which the ideal is brought to terms with the real world. In each of the novels of Henry Green, with one or two exceptions, an ideal is submitted or an unreal ecstasy is described; then later, there are experiences in the real world which contain recognizable features from the ideal or ecstasy, compromised and distorted though they may be.

The initial presentation may simply be an abstract statement of an ideal; but, more fascinating, it may be a pictorial representation. The latter is frequently one long sinewy sentence, made up of richly sensuous images with more than usual intensity of color and texture and less than the usual amount of syntax to link them together. Such a style provides a vivid picture, stylized out of nature.

It may be a memory of childhood or youth, edited and hence ideal, that appears first; or it may be a visionary dream of the future. Between these two kinds of ideal there is no essential difference; for that which comes edited from the past is still looked forward to as a future fulfillment, and the hope which sponsors a dream of the future is based on the supposition that there was once an ideal past.

In *Living* the statement of the ideal is not pictorialized. Lily's prayer is an abstract statement of an ideal projected into the future; and the future reproduces it nonpictorially with recognizable essentials shorn of ideality. There are one or two images of the south of France, the promised land, in *Party Going*. But the important ideal nursed by Julia is that of virginity; it is a nonregressive allurement, however, and she looks forward to its modification in the way of the world.

In *Blindness* there are some unnatural images of nature as remembered by the blind boy. But no parts of these images appear later, married to reality. The first significant presentation of an ecstasy in pictorial terms is in *Caught*. Richard Roe nurses the edited memory of his first love; and then later in the novel succeeds in bringing the garden imagery that attended it to his affair with his second love. In *Back*, the procedure by which the tension between ideality and the world is annihilated finds its fullest objectification. Charley Summers proceeds like Roe from one rose garden to another. But the technique in *Back* is somewhat different from that used in *Caught*. The first stylized, sensuous passage, which presents the graveyard, is not a literal description of the early love itself but a kind of metaphor for it, with the quality of death represented. Behind the metaphor is a fictional dream of sexual consummation. Then later there is another garden, partly reminiscent of the graveyard, where the living replaces the dead; and finally there is the real consummation of love, in a setting described in the imagery of roses.

The pictorialized ecstasy in *Nothing* bears a close relation to the analogues in *Caught* and *Back*. It is a beautiful, stylized, and innocent enactment of what is to come. It is not, however, an edited memory like Roe's, though we cannot be sure that it is not the metaphorical rendering of a memory, comparable with Charley's but departing somewhat farther from the real. Like the analogues described above, its earthly counterpart brings into reality important elements from the ecstasy.

In *Loving* the pictorial reality at the end of the novel reflects the early ecstasy in the library. But it reflects also an imaginary picture in Raunce's mind of a hypothetical, not an edited, scene of Edith kissing another man. Though analogous, the process is given a special complexity: the mental image is not described at all, but it is specifically designated "picture." The image differs from its analogues in that its ideality consists merely in the fact that Raunce never witnessed it with his outward senses; and again, it is unlike the pictures in the other novels since it is accompanied by fear. But we need not suppose that the fear is only or even chiefly due to a possible rivalry over Edith. The not unpalatable fear associated with the picture has been seen earlier in the novel; it is provoked by Edith's frightening sexual potentiality. Thus when the ecstasy is brought to reality and the picture is described, the fear that attended the original ideality is accordingly present again. Edith as terrible sexuality in ideal abstraction has become Edith as terrible sexuality in fact for Raunce.

In the analogues considered above, except the one in *Blindness,* both the initial dream and the action or situation in which the dream becomes real are sexual. Now sex in Green, as we have noted, is the means by which characters assert selfness and at the same time break out of alienation into community. In two novels, stylized descriptions which produce pictorialization are bestowed upon things that are not objects of sexuality. In *Doting* the juggler's act is pictorialized. Not in itself an object of sexuality it offers in unreality such a perfect ritualistic and dexterous management of sexual symbols as ought to have been brought to reality by Arthur Middleton. In *Concluding,* Mr. Rock's pig appears as a picture. It has no connection with sex but has a significant relatedness to community. For Mr. Rock's salvation, though not his selfcreation, lies in his supporting this and the other animals which stand between him and complete isolation.

Finally, the development of the style shows no greater step than that between *Blindness* and *Living,* already sufficiently discussed, by which commerce among words is replaced by commerce among referents. The technique of style in *Living* by which referents are presented in stark reality and the relationships between them tend to be erased is most remarkable in the later novels in passages describing ecstasies. For as these are memories untrammeled by constraints of necessity, so their luster need not be dimmed by the confinement of their *Dinglichkeit* in dull, routine syntax. After *Living,* style draws less attention to itself. But the control on words, which makes its conspicuous appearance in *Living,* is not subsequently relaxed and the choice of words is always precise.

Then more important to this study are the modifications in style and strategy, giving variety to the relationships of the parts to each other and to the whole. In summary these modifications may be discussed in terms used earlier: Coleridge's fancy and imagination, Ransom's texture and structure. In *Blindness,* the respect for the integrity of percepts which I associate with the mode of fancy makes an initial fleeting appearance. In *Living,,* the various small metaphors and, in *Party Going,* both the small ones and the large metaphor of the hotel work in the mode of fancy, and the integrity of percepts is not violated to make them serve a purpose alien to their own.

Caught, on the other hand, proceeds predominantly in the mode of the imagination, for the viewpoint has moved inside the mind of the protagonist; and percepts surrender themselves to be shaped according to the requirements of a function larger than and slightly different from the natural, individual function of each. But the procedure need not be regarded as comprehensive: there are many details presented with pure objectivity, and there are small matters, pursued for themselves alone, that are untroubled by autocratic treatment. The part of Pye's speech that has been quoted, for instance, succeeds in the end in making its own point, despite Pye's obsession which invades it; and then, on the other hand, the presence of loose sentences, for which the style of *Caught* is remarkable, may demonstrate to a limited degree the independence of independent matters. And that independence may be observed in all succeeding novels. But the operation of the imagination is evident also. Indeed, it must perforce be at work in all novels where ecstasies are recreated or where characters make their private symbols. Arthur Middleton's failure in *Doting* to recreate the ecstasy may perhaps be attributed to a lack of imagination as well as to clumsiness. In *Nothing,* imagination, associated with passion, is observed in Jane Weatherby; its absence in Philip constitutes a small villainy.

In *Concluding* and the novels following it, the relationship of the parts to the whole may be viewed as a conflict between texture and structure. From style, which might choose between fancy and imagination as the controlling faculty in the creation, our interest turns to strategy, which may support texture or structure. In *Concluding,* the texture is at large. But the constraining factor here, the structure, is not that relatively benevolent shaping spirit of the imagination that violates merely the definite outline of individual sensous perceptions; it is that scientific rule that virtually denies individuality altogether. The structure of *Nothing* and *Doting* is less rigid. And it is democratic, for texture itself contributes to its strength.

Style and strategy then side with content; imagery is liberated by the fancy, not controlled by the imagination, and texture is awarded its due *Dinglichkeit* and forces its claims, if necessary, at the cost of impairing structure; in the content, individual people work out their individual salvation in defiance, if necessary, of organized opposition. This fidelity toward entity rather than system or mass may not easily be called exceptional. For there is no end to the novels, dramas, and poems, especially in this age, that explore the theme of the one against the many and side with the one. And further, if such a fidelity is not indeed one of the general conditions of all art, it is at least the important means by which art escapes being sociology.

But, although this consideration is duly sobering, Green's fidelity to entity still seems remarkable. First, it has an additional dimension in that it controls not only content but style and strategy. Then, since self-creation is being explored, emphasis tends to fall on the private, nonrepresentative experiences of protagonists as it does not, or at least need not, in other works concerned with the one against the many. We should never deduce from the novels of Henry Green the doctrine that particularity leads to universality. This is not to say that in Green as elsewhere unique characters in their unique situations may not develop representative tensions and feelings. Each man, for instance, may at some time "come upon a place foreign to him but which he was aware he had to visit," and the arrival there of so many of Green's characters may be considered representative. But then if, in this instance, the representative archetypal circumstance is discernible back of the unique variations, the nightmare undergone by the individual characters within that strange place is perfectly peculiar to each and not extensible. And while the fact of the strangeness may be representative, it is rather the unsharable terms of the strangeness, the terms of suffering peculiar in each individual, that the novels tend to dwell on.

There is another widespread and generally unsharable feature of the novels: those tiny, anecdotal incidents, which appear to be true since they are too strange for fiction, that are perfectly unique and may never refer the reader to anything comparable in his own experience, but which he willingly accepts, understanding that Green's whole cosmos tends to be private. Among other small details, there is the raincoat which is eaten by pigs while its owner is up a ladder gathering apples; there is the woman whose lover has carved his initials low down on her back with an electric wire; and there are the servants who ask for money to go back to Italy to vote.

Then we note also a consonant playing down of backgrounds. When we read the general situations that provide backdrops in Green, our major reaction is not usually, "This is how it was" (except insofar as a scene serves as an objective correlative for private feelings, a relationship that this line of Hemingway's may itself *in situ* indicate). For, as with persons so with their environments, Green tends to back away from the representative picture and the general law of averages that governs it into the private recesses of individuality where unique laws are at work. He *tends* to do so. There are the novels in which time and place are deliberately obscured: the ethos is therefore prevented from being representative. Even in *Caught* and *Back,* which are both set in Greater London at specific times, the regard the novels pay to their backgrounds must not be overemphasized. It is true that *Caught* recalls the war and not just in occasional poignant details; but not one London street, or a single building, or any bridge, the names of all of which are so powerfully evocative of 1940, is specifically identified. For the story exists not primarily for the ethos but for Richard Roe, who is not primarily a child of it. Again, in *Back* no restaurant, no district, no railway station is named. Nor surely would any reader find in Charley Summers the representative of the type of men returned from the war; for what he is back from is something altogether individual; although, as suggested in my last paragraph, the fact of his sense of strangeness, the fact of his fears, and so on, may be representative. It is significant that these two novels set in specific place and time are the two that, more than any others, show the imagination at work. For by means of this faculty, place and time render up their autonomy in order that they may minister to the far more important autonomy of the protagonist. London virtually ceases to be London; time does not matter. The nature of the ethos, the enveloping mass, has been constrained to conform to the nature of an entity within it.

It is Henry Green's "villains" who tend to view persons in the mass, as fractions contributory to an ism statistically greater than themselves. So Mrs. Tennant, in *Loving,* considers the servants as homogeneous; James Phillips, in *Back,* feeds on abstracts; Miss Edge, in *Concluding,* is notoriously thorough in her refusal to see individuals as individuals; Philip Weatherby, in *Nothing,* thinks largely in terms of national issues. Opposed to these are ranged the characters who find people to be integers and, like the modern atomic scientist, regard the private living law of the individual rather than the "statistical" representative law of the mass: Raunce, who learns to love an individual; Charley Summers, who stands up for private concrete features; Mr. Rock, who discovers Moira as an entity; and Jane Weatherby, who loves little things.

Finally, in this connection, Green's exceptional fidelity to the small entity may have delayed his well-deserved popularity. For there is still a demand, though it is probably smaller than it has been, that the novel shall "say" something, or that it shall make clear where the author "stands." It may be that among readers there are too many Edges and Philip Weatherbys and too few entire men. For the entire man, according to William James, though he may temporarily tire of "the concrete clash and dust and pettiness" of the world, "will never carry the philosophic yoke upon his shoulders, and when tired of the grey monotony of her problems and insipid spaciousness of her results, will always gladly escape gleefully into the teeming and dramatic richness of the concrete world."[3] For such a world is that of Green's novels.

To the concretion of Henry Green's world I have paid tribute. I ought perhaps to conclude by reaffirming my awareness of its richness. Then, since it is rich, in order to do justice to its creator, in order rather to avoid doing injustice, the sequence of actions and suffering which constitutes the program for self-creation and which has been observed in the foregoing chapters may be regarded only as one imperfect theme. In this chapter

I have tried to press different features, as far as they ought
to be pressed, into a system. And the attempt is a relative
failure; for they go unwillingly, showing at the last moment
the idiosyncrasy, the special twist or facet which precludes
their categorization. Richness means complexity; and the
effort to make conclusions defeats itself, rather leading one
out into wider speculations. And so whatever system I may
have, it must be considered as offering only one reading, which
does not pretend to have tamed into regiment the total, vari-
egated, and spectacular wealth of the novels.

NOTES

Chapter 1

1. Edward Stokes's book, *The Novels of Henry Green* (London: The Hogarth Press, 1959), did not appear until this study was with the publisher, and I have therefore been unable to make use of it. Mr. Stokes's intentions are different from my own and, in some respects, so is his experience of the novels. But I am interested to note the consonance of certain of our observations, which are entirely independent.

Chapter 2

1. Henry Green, *Blindness* (London: J. M. Dent and Sons, 1926), p. 3.

2. *Ibid.*, p. 34.

3. *Ibid.*, p. 47.

4. *Ibid.*, p. 66.

5. *Ibid.*, p. 83.

6. *Ibid.*, p. 85.

7. *Ibid.*, p. 148.

8. *Ibid.*, p. 158.

9. *Ibid.*, p. 247.

10. Søren Kiekegaard, *The Concept of Dread,* trans. Walter Lowrie (Princeton: Princeton University Press, 1946), p. 139. See also Rollo May, *The Meaning of Anxiety* (New York: Ronald Press, 1950), pp. 27-45.

11. Kierkegaard, *The Concept of Dread,* p. 139.

12. Jean-Paul Sartre, *Being and Nothingness: An Essay on Phenomenological Ontology,* trans. Hazel E. Barnes (New York: Philosophical Library, 1956), p. 29.

13. *Blindness,* p. 7.

14. Kierkegaard, *The Concept of Dread,* p. 92.

157

158   Notes

15. *Blindness,* p. 202.
16. *Ibid.,* p. 68. Italics mine.
17. *Ibid.,* p. 62.
18. *Ibid.,* p. 77.
19. *Ibid.,* p. 243.
20. *Ibid.,* p. 242.
21. Kierkegaard, *The Concept of Dread,* p. 96.
22. Lionel Trilling, *The Liberal Imagination: Essays on Literature and Society* (New York: Doubleday and Co., 1950), p. 164.
23. *Blindness,* p. 148.
24. *Ibid.,* p. 151.
25. *Ibid.,* p. 250.
26. *Ibid.,* pp. 252-53.
27. *Ibid.,* p. 114.
28. See Nathan A. Scott, *Rehearsals of Discomposure: Alienation and Reconciliation in Modern Literature: Franz Kafka, Ignazio Silone, D. H. Lawrence, T. S. Eliot* (New York: King's Crown Press, 1952), pp. 48 ff.
29. *Ibid.,* pp. 5 ff.
30. *Forces in Modern British Literature: 1885-1956* (New York: Alfred A. Knopf, 1956), p. 148.
31. Scott, *Rehearsals of Discomposure.*
32. Kierkegaard, *The Concept of Dread,* pp. 110-11.
33. *Blindness,* p. 111. Italics mine.

Chapter 3
1. Henry Green, *Living* (London: The Hogarth Press, 1953), p. 209.
2. *Ibid.,* p. 45.
3. *Ibid.,* p. 245.
4. *Ibid.,* p. 268.
5. *Ibid.,* pp. 75-76.
6. *Ibid.,* p. 78.
7. *Ibid.,* p. 109. The cry is almost identical with that of D. H. Lawrence's male Lily in *Aaron's Rod.*
8. *Ibid.,* pp. 109-10.
9. *Ibid.,* pp. 228-29.
10. *Ibid.,* p. 62.
11. *Ibid.,* p. 111.
12. *Ibid.,* pp. 217-18.
13. Compare Edward Stokes, who finds that the pigeons in *Living* "render the quality of thought and feeling of the chief characters. The pigeons come to symbolize the complex, contradictory desires of the characters" ("Henry Green, Dispossessed Poet," *Australian Quarterly,* XXVIII [December, 1956], 89).
14. *Living,* p. 170.
15. *Ibid.,* pp. 105-6.

16. Henry Green, *Blindness* (London: J. M. Dent and Sons, 1926), p. 66.

17. The adjective is from Walter Allen: "Rupert Brooke is just round the corner and John Drinkwater may drop in at any moment" ("An Artist of the Thirties," *Folios of New Writing*, Spring, 1941, p. 152). The style of *Blindness* may perhaps be said to image "romanticism in decline," under the shadow of which Cyril Connolly, who was at Eton with Green, says he grew up (*Enemies of Promise* [New York: The Macmillan Co., 1948], p. 169).

18. Henry Green, *Pack My Bag* (London: The Hogarth Press, 1952), pp. 163-64 and 191-92, respectively.

19. Henry Green, *Blindness,* pp. 151 ff. Italics mine.

20. Henry Green, *Pack My Bag,* p. 88.

21. Philip Toynbee attributes the modifications of conventional English prose in *Living* simply to an aversion to its looseness ("The Novels of Henry Green," *Partisan Review,* XVI [May, 1949], 492).

22. Giorgio Melchiori attributes the abolition of the definite article to the influence of Auden *(The Tightrope Walkers: Studies of Mannerism in Modern English Literature* [London: Routledge and Kegan Paul, 1956], p. 192).

23. See Melchiori (*ibid.*, p. 193), who compares Green's style with impressionism where "the simplification of natural forms" heightens "the emotional quality of the picture by concentrating on the really significant features."

24. See Freud on the absence of logical relationships in dreams (*Basic Writings of Sigmund Freud,* ed. and trans. A. A. Brill [New York: Random House, 1938], pp. 342 ff.).

25. *Living,* p. 167.

26. I take these visual images to reflect the mood of the girl Hannah and not that of the author. Melchiori (*The Tightrope Walkers,* p. 194) finds that "visual images without an abstract counterpart in the realm of thought or a definite reference to known facts or persons are the expression only of a mood, of a condition of the author's mind, so individual that it can be communicated only through visual embodiment."

27. *Living,* p. 26.

28. *Ibid.,* p. 32.

29. *Ibid.,* p. 63.

30. *Ibid.,* p. 122.

31. *Ibid.,* p. 147.

32. *Ibid.,* pp. 131-32.

33. *Ibid.,* pp. 6-7.

Chapter 4

1. Henry Green, *Party Going* (London: The Hogarth Press, 1951), p. 39.

2. Henry Green, "Mr. Jonas," *Folios of New Writing*, Spring, 1941, pp. 11-12.

3. *Party Going*, pp. 15-16.

4. *Ibid.*, p. 59.

5. Robert Penn Warren, *World Enough and Time* (New York: Random House, 1950), p. 312.

6. Ignazio Silone, *The Seed Beneath the Snow*, trans. Frances Frenaye (New York: Harper and Bros., 1942), p. 49.

7. Albert Camus, *The Stranger*, trans. Stuart Gilbert (New York: Alfred A. Knopf, 1957), pp. 153-54.

8. Giorgio Melchiori (*The Tightrope Walkers: Studies of Mannerism in Modern English Literature* [London: Routledge and Kegan Paul, 1956], p. 200) finds the "real subject" of *Party Going*, as well as of *Caught* and *Loving*, to be "the emotional impact of waiting," citing Henry Reed (*The Novel Since 1939* [London: Longmans, Green and Co., 1949], p. 29), who describes all three as "emotional black holes of Calcutta."

9. *Party Going*, p. 201.

10. *Ibid.*, p. 79.

11. *Ibid.*, p. 224.

12. *Ibid.*, p. 72.

13. *Ibid.*, p. 203.

14. Jean-Paul Sartre, *Being and Nothingness: An Essay on Phenomenological Ontology*, trans. Hazel E. Barnes (New York: Philosophical Library, 1956), p. 364.

15. *Party Going*, p. 215.

16. *Ibid.*, p. 255. Italics mine.

17. Walter Allen, "An Artist of the Thirties," *Folios of New Writing*, Spring, 1941, p. 155.

18. As did the reviewers of *Blindness* in 1926. The writer of the unsigned article, "Fiction" (*Saturday Review of Literature*, III [December 25, 1926], 472), finds the entire book, except for its opening section, to consist of variations and restatements of a single theme—blindness, from the viewpoint of the blind. Another reviewer, D. B. W. ("Recent Fiction," *New Republic*, XLIX [December 29, 1926], 174), finds in the novel "the very inner sense of the experience of blindness suffered by a person naturally hypersensitive to beauty."

19. Readings that discover social significance in *Party Going* are offered by Edward Stokes ("Henry Green, Dispossessed Poet," *Australian Quarterly*, XXVIII [December, 1956], 84-91), who finds that "The railway station . . . is a symbol of the whole rickety social structure"; by Bruce Bain ("Henry Green: The Man and His Work," *World Review*, [May, 1949], p. 56), who finds the book "a suggestive allegory of the position of the English privileged class, whose style of living is lightly but brilliantly pilloried"; and by Walter Allen ("Henry Green," *Penguin New Writing*, XXV [1945], 151), who finds

Party Going a satire on people with wealth but without responsibility.
20. Their very felicity may be an obscuring factor. We fail to question whether faith, in Arnold's poem, has any aspects *not* like the sea; or whether in the New Testament, the Holy Ghost has any attributes that *pneuma* does not suggest. We are better off when the poet tests his metaphor before our eyes and points out its limitations as Shakespeare does in Sonnet 16.
21. Samuel Taylor Coleridge, *Biographia Literaria* (London: J. M. Dent and Sons, 1947), p. 43. I have italicized the adverbs.
22. *Ibid.*, p. 49.
23. "Donne and the Rhetorical Tradition," *Kenyon Review*, XI (Autumn, 1949), 580.
24. *Party Going*, p. 196.
25. *Ibid.*, pp. 201-2.
26. *Ibid.*, p. 59.
27. *Ibid.*, p. 29.
28. *Ibid.*, p. 7.
29. *Ibid.*, p. 97.

Chapter 5
1. See Rollo May, *The Meaning of Anxiety* (New York: The Ronald Press, 1950), p. 38.
2. Henry Green, *Caught* (London: The Hogarth Press, 1952), p. 32.
3. *Ibid.*, p. 9.
4. *Ibid.*, p. 178. In the discussion of the garden my indebtedness to Robert Penn Warren (see especially "Pure and Impure Poetry," *Essays in Modern Literary Criticism*, ed. Ray B. West, Jr. [New York: Rinehart and Co., 1952], pp. 246-66) is perfectly apparent.
5. *Ibid.*, p. 64.
6. *Ibid.*, p. 65.
7. Søren Kierkegaard, *The Concept of Dread*, trans. Walter Lowrie (Princeton: Princeton University Press, 1946), p. 58.
8. *Caught*, pp. 50-51.
9. *Ibid.*, p. 108.
10. *Ibid.*, p. 111.
11. *Ibid.*, p. 120. Italics mine.
12. *Ibid.*, p. 9.
13. Pure objectivity may not, of course, be achieved by the artist. Henry Green makes the point himself in a Third Programme broadcast *(Listener*, November 9, 1950, pp. 505-6).
14. *Caught*, p. 49.
15. I wish to refine Walter Allen's description of the novel, "the incomprehension and incommunicability of Kafka played out in a naturalistic setting" ("Henry Green," *Penguin New Writing*, XXV [1945], 152-53).
16. In positing a "main character" and in my following treatment

of him, I differ from Edward Stokes who finds such a character only in *Back*, which he considers "unique among Green's novels in keeping close throughout to the nerves and consciousness of one character, Charley Summers" ("Henry Green, Dispossessed Poet," *Australian Quarterly*, XXVIII [December, 1956], 87).

17. Samuel Johnson, "Milton," *Lives of the English Poets* (London: J. M. Dent and Sons, 1946), I, 97.

18. *Caught*, p. 53.

19. *Ibid.*, p. 37.

20. *Ibid.*, p. 48.

21. *Ibid.*, p. 49.

22. Sigmund Freud, "The Interpretation of Dreams," *The Basic Writings of Sigmund Freud*, trans. A. A. Brill (New York: Random House, 1938), p. 238.

23. *Ibid.*, p. 349.

24. Dorothy Van Ghent, *The English Novel: Form and Function* (New York: Rinehart and Co., 1953), p. 133.

25. Henry Green, *Party Going* (London: The Hogarth Press, 1950), p. 95.

26. *Caught*, p. 119.

27. *Ibid.*, p. 66.

28. *Basic Writings*, pp. 222-23.

29. *Caught*, p. 175.

30. *Ibid.*, p. 178.

31. *Ibid.*, p. 179.

32. See Henry Green, "A Novelist to His Readers," *Listener*, November 9, 1950, p. 505.

33. *Caught*, pp. 176, 180.

34. *Ibid.*, p. 180.

35. *Ibid.*

36. See Nigel Dennis, "The Double Life of Henry Green," *Life*, August 4, 1952, p. 94. Compare in *Blindness*, John Haye's description of his diary as "just a sort of pipe to draw off the swamp water."

37. *Caught*, p. 176.

38. *Ibid.*, p. 194.

39. *Ibid.*, p. 117.

Chapter 6

1. Henry Green, *Loving* (New York: Viking Press, 1949), p. 13.

2. Søren Kierkegaard, "Problem I," *Fear and Trembling*, trans. Walter Lowrie (New York: Doubleday and Co., 1954), pp. 64-77. See also Nathan A. Scott, *Rehearsals of Discomposure: Alienation and Reconciliation in Modern Literature: Franz Kafka, Ignazio Silone, D. H. Lawrence, T. S. Eliot* (New York: King's Crown Press, 1952), pp. 53 ff.

3. *Loving*, p. 13.

4. *Ibid.*, p. 65.

5. *Ibid.*, p. 85.

6. See John Crowe Ransom, *God without Thunder* (New York: Harcourt Brace, 1930), p. 137.

7. See Jean-Paul Sartre, *Being and Nothingness: An Essay in Phenomenological Ontology*, trans. Hazel E. Barnes (New York: Philosophical Library, 1956), pp. 259 ff.

8. *Ibid.*, p. 364.

9. *Loving*, pp. 84-85.

10. *Ibid.*, pp. 215-16.

11. *Ibid.*, p. 153.

12. *Ibid.*, p. 248.

13. *Ibid.*, p. 207.

14. Henry Reed, *The Novel Since 1939* (London: Longmans, Green and Co., 1949), p. 87.

15. Giorgio Melchiori, *The Tightrope Walkers: Studies of Mannerism in Modern English Literature* (London: Routledge and Kegan Paul, 1956), p. 202.

16. *Loving*, p. 176.

17. James Hall, "The Fiction of Henry Green: Paradoxes of Pleasure-Pain," *Kenyon Review*, XIX (Winter, 1957), 76. I have not noted every instance of my indebtedness to this perceptive article.

18. *Loving*, p. 230.

19. Henry Green, "A propos du roman non representatif," *Roman*, June, 1951, p. 243: "Il semble bien qu'après trois guerres, en comptant la guerre des Boers, en cinquante ans, et une guerre froide par là-dessus, avec tous les revers de fortune individuels provoqués par ces bouleversements, sans parler des révolutions qui ont en lieu dans l'intervalle, le lecteur en ait assez des désastres personnels."

20. *Loving*, p. 213.

21. Henry Green, "A Novelist to His Readers," *Listener*, November 9, 1950, pp. 505-6.

22. *Loving*, p. 135.

23. *Ibid.*, p. 106.

24. *Ibid.*, p. 243.

25. *Ibid.*, p. 137.

26. *Ibid.*, p. 67.

27. *Ibid.*, p. 163.

Chapter 7

1. Henry Green, "The Lull," *New Writing and Daylight*, Summer, 1943, pp. 11-21.

2. Henry Green, *Back* (London: The Hogarth Press, 1951), p. 13.

3. James Hall, "The Fiction of Henry Green: Paradoxes of Pleasure-Pain," *Kenyon Review*, XIX (Winter, 1957), 76.

4. Henry Green, *Caught* (London: The Hogarth Press, 1952), pp. 23-24.

5. Samuel Taylor Coleridge, *Biographia Literaria* (London: J. M. Dent and Sons, 1947), p. 43.

6. *Back,* p. 122. Italics mine.

7. *Ibid.,* pp. 146-47.

8. *Ibid.,* p. 134.

9. *Ibid.*

10. *Ibid.,* p. 128.

11. *Ibid.,* p. 129.

12. Ernest Hemingway, *A Farewell to Arms* (New York: Charles Scribner's Sons, 1957), p. 191.

13. Ignazio Silone, *Bread and Wine,* trans. Gwenda David and Eric Mosbacher (New York: Harper and Bros., 1946), p. 158.

14. *Ibid.,* p. 207.

15. *Back,* p. 89.

Chapter 8

1. Henry Green, *Back* (London: The Hogarth Press, 1951), p. 6.

2. *Ibid.,* pp. 9-10.

3. *Ibid.,* p. 87.

4. See Bruce Bain, who considers the coincidence of their similarity "too clumsy as a dramatic peg, too glib as a symbol" ("Henry Green: The Man and His Work," *World Review* [May, 1949], p. 58).

5. *Ibid.*

6. James Hall, "The Fiction of Henry Green: Paradoxes of Pleasure-Pain," *Kenyon Review,* XIX (Winter, 1957), 76.

7. Henry Green, *Concluding* (London: The Hogarth Press, 1959), p. 19.

8. *Ibid.,* p. 99.

9. *Ibid.,* p. 92.

10. *Ibid.,* p. 199.

11. Hall, p. 76.

12. The state in *Concluding,* of course, is not communist. It shares with communism the atheism, seen in the formula used for grace after meals, and the jargon. The state car, colored red, is reminiscent, not of communism but of English post office vehicles and letter boxes. The state here is the creation of no particular ism. As C. S. Lewis says (writing during the war against Fascism), "the process which, if not checked, will abolish man, goes on apace among Communists and Democrats no less than among Fascists" (*The Abolition of Man* [London: Geoffrey Bles, 1947]), pp. 50-51.

13. *Concluding,* p. 213.

14. *Ibid.,* p. 56.

15. *Ibid.,* p. 48.

16. *Ibid.,* pp. 81, 82.

17. *Ibid.,* p. 8.

18. *Ibid.,* p. 98.

19. *Ibid.*, p. 99.
20. *Ibid.*, p. 177.
21. *Ibid.*, p. 187.
22. *Ibid.*, p. 175.
23. Mark Schorer describes the sensuality in *Concluding* as "self-corrupting" ("The Real and Unreal Worlds of Henry Green," *New York Herald Tribune Book Review*, December 31, 1950, p. 5).
24. *Concluding*, p. 85.
25. *Ibid.*, p. 146.
26. *Ibid.*, p. 150.
27. *Ibid.*, p. 225.
28. *Ibid.*, p. 59.
29. *Ibid.*, p. 42.
30. *Ibid.*, p. 206.
31. *Ibid.*, p. 37.
32. *Ibid.*, p. 8.
33. *Ibid.*, p. 151.
34. *Ibid.*, p. 157.
35. *Ibid.*, p. 13.
36. *Ibid.*, p. 14. "Did'nt" for "didn't" is Green's usage.
37. *Ibid.*, p. 18.
38. *Ibid.*, p. 241.
39. *Ibid.*, pp. 205, 88, and 33, respectively.
40. *Ibid.*, pp. 60 and 62, respectively.
41. Philip Toynbee, "The Novels of Henry Green," *Partisan Review*, XVI (1949), 496.
42. John Crowe Ransom, *The World's Body* (New York: Charles Scribner's Sons, 1938), pp. 112-42.
43. John Crowe Ransom, "Criticism as Pure Speculation," *The Intent of the Critic,* ed. Donald A. Stauffer (Princeton: Princeton University Press, 1941), p. 108.
44. The close marriage of form and content is discussed by Robert Phelps ("The Vision of Henry Green,"*Hudson Review,*V [Winter, 1953], 614-20), who discovers, for example, that Raunce and Edith, in *Loving,* "persuade the final sentence of the book to abet them by assuring us that 'over in England they were married and lived happily ever after.'"
45. *Concluding*, p. 47.
46. *Ibid.*, p. 55.
47. *Ibid.*, p. 61.
48. *Ibid.*, p. 96.

Chapter 9
1. Ernest Jones, "Henry Green, Virtuoso," *Nation*, November 8, 1950, p. 328.
2. Henry Green, *Nothing* (New York: Viking Press, 1950), p. 13. Italics mine.

3. *Ibid.*, pp. 79-80.
4. *Ibid.*, p. 121.
5. *Ibid.*, p. 75.
6. *Ibid.*, pp. 34-35.
7. *Ibid.*, p. 160.
8. *Ibid.*, p. 242.
9. *Ibid.*, pp. 246-47.
10. *Ibid.*, p. 55.
11. *Ibid.*, p. 173.
12. *Ibid.*, p. 188.
13. *Ibid.*, p. 84.
14. *Ibid.*, p. 122.
15. *Ibid.*, p. 71.
16. *Ibid.*, p. 78.
17. *Ibid.*, p. 71.
18. *Ibid.*, p. 76.
19. *Ibid.*, pp. 11-12.
20. *Ibid.*, p. 13.
21. *Ibid.*, p. 119.
22. Ernest Jones, "Henry Green, Virtuoso," p. 329.
23. Henry Green, *Doting* (London: The Hogarth Press, 1952), pp. 162 ff. and 177 ff.
24. *Ibid.*, p. 101.
25. *Ibid.*, p. 89.
26. *Ibid.*, p. 1.
27. *Ibid.*, p. 54.
28. *Ibid.*, p. 4.
29. *Ibid.*, p. 7.
30. *Ibid.*, p. 21.
31. *Ibid.*, p. 153.
32. *Ibid.*, p. 111.
33. *Ibid.*, p. 8.
34. *Ibid.*, p. 13.
35. *Ibid.*, p. 39.
36. *Ibid.*, p. 25.
37. *Ibid.*, pp. 58-59.
38. *Ibid.*, p. 53.
39. *Ibid.*, p. 6.
40. See James Hall, "The Fiction of Henry Green: Paradoxes of Pleasure-Pain," *Kenyon Review,* XIX (Winter, 1957), 76 ff.
41. *Doting,* p. 252.

Chapter 10
1. Brendan Gill, "Something," *New Yorker,* March 25, 1950, p. 112.

2. This aspect of various of Green's novels is perceptively discussed by Robert Phelps, "The Vision of Henry Green," *Hudson Review,* V (Winter, 1953), 614-20.

3. William James, *Essays in Pragmatism* (New York: Hafner Library of Classics, 1955), p. 7.

BIBLIOGRAPHY

WORKS OF HENRY GREEN

First English and First American Editions

Blindness. London: J. M. Dent, 1926; New York: E. P. Dutton, 1926.
Living. London: Hogarth, 1929.
Party Going. London: Hogarth, 1939; New York: Viking, 1951.
Pack My Bag. London: Hogarth, 1940.
Caught. London: Hogarth, 1943; New York: Viking, 1950.
Loving. London: Hogarth, 1945; New York: Viking, 1949.
Back. London: Hogarth, 1946; New York: Viking, 1950.
Concluding. London: Hogarth, 1948; New York: Viking, 1950.
Nothing. London: Hogarth, 1950; New York: Viking, 1950.
Doting. London: Hogarth, 1952; New York: Viking, 1952.

Selected Short Works

"Mr. Jonas," *Folios of New Writing*, Spring, 1941, pp. 11-16.
"The Lull," *New Writing and Daylight*, Summer, 1943, pp. 11-21.
"A Novelist to His Readers," *The Listener*, November 9, 1950, pp. 505-6.
"A propos du roman non representatif," *Roman*, June, 1951, pp. 238-45.

CRITICAL WORKS ABOUT HENRY GREEN

Allen, Walter. "An Artist of the Thirties," *Folios of New Writing*, Spring, 1941, pp. 149-58.
—————. "Henry Green," *Penguin New Writing*, 1945, pp. 144-55.
Anonymous. "Fiction," *The Saturday Review of Literature*, III (December 25, 1926), 472.

Bain, Bruce. "Henry Green: The Man and His Work," *World Review,* May, 1949, pp. 55-58, 80.

D. B. W. "Recent Fiction," *The New Republic,* XLIV (December 29, 1926), 174.

Dennis, Nigel. "The Double Life of Henry Green," *Life,* August 4, 1952, pp. 83-94.

Gill, Brendan. "Something," *The New Yorker,* March 25, 1950, pp. 111-12.

Hall, James. "The Fiction of Henry Green: Paradoxes of Pleasure-Pain," *The Kenyon Review,* XIX (Winter, 1957), 76-88.

Jones, Ernest. "Henry Green, Virtuoso," *The Nation,* November 8, 1950, pp. 328-29.

Melchiori, Giorgio. *The Tightrope Walkers: Essays on Mannerism in Modern English Literature.* London: Routledge and Paul, 1956.

Phelps, Robert. "The Vision of Henry Green," *The Hudson Review,* V (Winter, 1953), 614-20.

Reed, Henry. *The Novel Since 1939.* London: Phoenix House, 1949.

Schorer, Mark. "The Real and Unreal Worlds of Henry Green," *The New York Herald Tribune Book Review,* December 31, 1950, p. 5.

Stokes, Edward. "Henry Green, Dispossessed Poet," *The Australian Quarterly,* XXVIII (December, 1956), 84-91.

Tindall, William York. *Forces in Modern British Literature 1885-1956.* New York: Knopf, 1956.

Toynbee, Philip. "The Novels of Henry Green," *The Partisan Review,* XVI (May, 1949), 487-97.